Harley's Story

The Life Of An Addict

C.J. Levan

ISBN 978-1-64416-475-4 (paperback)
ISBN 978-1-64416-559-1 (hardcover)
ISBN 978-1-64416-477-8 (digital)

Christian Faith Publishing, Inc.
832 Park Avenue
Meadville, PA 16335
www.christianfaithpublishing.com

Printed in the United States of America

In loving memory of my beautiful daughter
Harley Lynn Harlan (7/1/90–12/21/16)

I feel compelled to put my baby's story out there in hopes of helping struggling addicts and their loved ones better cope with the utter destruction of drug addiction and the devastating aftermath.

Chapter

1

This is Harley's story, but in telling it, I should first give you some insight into mine. I need to more or less start at the beginning so you are better able to understand how certain situations and circumstances may have had a profound effect on shaping her life and everyone around her.

I often said to her, "After seeing all that I had gone through, why would you go down the same path?" To which she would reply, "Yeah, you'd think I would have run the other way."

They say children of addicts often grow up to become addicts themselves. I guess there is some truth to that a lot of times.

So to begin . . .

I started smoking weed at sixteen and before long was experimenting with every other drug that was out there at the time: LSD, quaaludes, speed, angel dust, to name a few. I foolishly got married right after graduating from high school, and gave birth to my first daughter soon after. That marriage lasted just under a year—a whole eleven months.

When my daughter was two, I met my son's father, whom I was with for five years. My son came along when my daughter was four. That relationship soon dissolved, and for the next six years, I was raising two children on my own, all while continuing the drug use and the drinking nonstop.

Somehow I was able to hold down a full-time job. I was a functioning addict/alcoholic and always thought despite it all, I was a good mother. I always kept a clean house and had home-made meals on the table. I would take the kids to places and do things with them on my days off. My dad and I were always really close, and I remember him telling me how proud he was of me. When the kids told my parents about the drugs (kids aren't dumb, no matter how you try to hide it), he took me out to dinner and offered to get me help. By then, my drug of choice was cocaine. I thanked him but sadly turned him down. I didn't want help. I liked it too much and didn't want to quit. It got to the point where I was using and drinking all day long, every day. For me, the two went together.

Chapter

2

It wasn't long before I was so into my addiction that I was working solely to pay for my habit.

My parents were my landlords, and after all that they had done for me, I even stopped paying my rent and all my other bills. Every cent I earned went to my addiction.

I met Harley's dad at a bar one night, and within a week or two, he had moved in with me. He was also an alcoholic and drug addict. One night, we talked about having a child together, and I stopped taking the pill.

The day after I told him that I suspected I was pregnant, I came home from work to find he had moved out. The next time I talked to him, he claimed not to remember that certain conversation (he was too coked up). He told me to have an abortion. I said no. I really want this baby.

I was devastated when he walked out; I was so in love with him. My mind-set at that point was if he doesn't care, why should I? I just kept on in a downward spiral. The drugs and the alcohol were a constant in my life, the whole way through my pregnancy. My son told my mother there isn't going to be a baby.

Harley's dad's mother prayed for me over the phone one night that God would lift the drugs away from this baby, and I believed with all my heart that he did just that. She was born on July 1, 1990—a perfect a beautiful little girl. She was premature, five weeks early, my little Cabbage Patch kid, weighing in at 4 pounds, 4 ounces. She actually wore a tiny robe from her big sister's doll.

She was always such a good and happy baby, a real joy. My dad called her his motorcycle kid. Her dad's mother would tell her one day she would meet and marry a man named Davidson, and she would be Harley Davidson.

Eight months later, her dad's new girlfriend also gave birth to a little girl, Macey. Betty and Bob (Harley's dad's parents) would have the two of them over on weekends to play together, so they would grow up knowing each other.

When Harley was three, I lost my job due to my addiction. Too much of being up all night and sleeping all day. I ended up going on welfare, and around the same time, my dad was diagnosed with Parkinson's disease. He never even got to enjoy retirement. It got to the point where my mom had to sell my house to pay all the medical bills and I moved into low-income housing.

By that time, my oldest daughter was living with my parents and my son wanted to live with his dad, so it was just Harley and I. By then, I was in an extremely abusive relationship with yet another man, and although he lived with us, he wasn't on the lease. He would just snap out of nowhere, and I was terrified that if I kicked him out he would burn the house down, or worse. I was finally able to get away from him after he broke my jaw and stole my car. Needless to say, he went to jail.

We lost my dad soon after, and I really went off the deep end. As it turned out, he was misdiagnosed. He never had Parkinson's. The medication was what killed him, at sixty-four years young.

I grew up in a Christian home with the best parents a kid could ask for. They gave my brother and I a wonderful life. We went on vacations to a different state every year, so there are very few I haven't seen. When I was twelve, we lived on the French Riviera. We traveled all over Europe on the weekends when Dad wasn't working.

Chapter

3

So getting back to Harley and I. She was four when we lost Dad. She was the most loving, giving, sweetest little girl. She would crawl into bed with me every morning and say, "Good morning, Mommy. I'm up." And we would just snuggle till I was ready to get up. She loved backrubs that I would give her every night while watching television, and when she had enough, she would roll over and say, "Okay, Mommy, belly rub."

She loved the *The Little Mermaid* video and Barney, to name a few. When I would tuck her in at night, we would sing the Barney song together: "I love you, you love me, we're a happy family." Then she would sing the Spanish version from the movie. Needless to say, she sang that part solo. I never mastered that, and it would always amaze me. She always seemed so happy.

That Easter, I took her on an egg hunt, and she did really well. I was pointing out some spots after she had found a lot on her own, and she said, "That's okay, Mommy. I have enough." What kid says that?

Another thing I will never forget is going upstairs to the bathroom while she was in her room playing. I stopped to watch her, and there she was standing in front of her toy box, looking in. She started digging, obviously looking for something and getting frustrated. She straightened up, put her little hands on her hips, and said, "Dammit!" It was then that she saw me, and she said, "Oops, sorry, Mommy."

Chapter

4

As I said, my dad passed away, and by that time, I was shooting up—something I told myself I would never do. I had two "friends" stop over one night, and the woman was always saying how I was always doing "baby shots" and decided to give me a bigger one. I came out of the bathroom thinking the smoke alarm was going off. I later found out it was an "ear ringer" from the coke.

I was shaking like a leaf, and Harley sensed there was something wrong. She started crying, and I was in no shape to go to her. These friends tried to calm her down, and told her, "Your mommy will be okay." They stayed with me until I was. I know now I was very close to OD-ing that night and my baby was right there. How could I have let my child see something like that?

I was always drinking and getting high, I never let up. I wanted to be numb then more than ever now that I had lost my dad. My mom lost the love of her life, and I was never there for her or my brother. To make matters even worse, on the heels of losing my dad (the one who was always there for me no matter what), Harley's grandparents forced me into a court-ordered rehab with the stipulation that if I completed it and anything else recommended, that I would get my little girl back. They had already taken me to court and were awarded partial custody. If I didn't complete the program, they intended to go for full custody.

Chapter

5

I lost our apartment, but because I was working through a temp agency by then, I had money for a motel room. All our things went into storage. I put off checking myself into rehab till I got good and drunk one night and made up my mind I had to do this. There was no way I was going to lose my baby!

My son, who was twelve at the time, was still with his dad, and my oldest daughter, now sixteen, had to go into a group home. It got to the point where my mother couldn't handle her anymore; with my dad gone and my daughter being a rebellious teenager, it was too much. She had moved back in with Harley and me. The judge wouldn't let her stay with her dad and his girlfriend because they only had one bedroom. She ran away from the home twice, and the judge then agreed to let her go with her dad.

By the time I was ordered into rehab, I had already been arrested twice and spent some time in the county jail for a drug sale (weed) and a DUI. I didn't want to get clean, I was only playing their game so I wouldn't lose my daughter, too stupid to see that I was setting myself up to fail.

A few days before I would've completed the thirty-day program, my counselor dropped a bombshell, telling me she was recommending an additional six months in a halfway house. I told her to shove it, I wasn't going, until she reminded me that I wouldn't get Harley back unless I did.

There was a two-week waiting period till they found me a bed, so they put me up in a recovery house in the same town I had been using in all those years. I knew Betty and Bob were just waiting for me to slip up, and I was determined not to give them the satisfaction if it killed me!

Betty brought Harley over to visit me, and later to the halfway house as well. I hated them for what they were doing, but they had her best interests at heart and never kept me from seeing her as long as they were there, which I resented even more.

Chapter

6

The halfway house was ten times worse than rehab, I couldn't do anything right. They nitpicked about every little thing! I loved to read, and they wouldn't let me, claiming it was my way of escaping.

One night, a friend I knew from the rehab and me were putting a puzzle together in the dining room. We were snacking on port wine cheese and crackers when the housemother came in and blew a gasket. She demanded to know where it came from and said I had to throw it out. I had brought it from home, and it had been in the community refrigerator for weeks.

Then came a day we had to make a poster cutting out pictures and words from magazines that best described our addiction. I had a pen that looked like a syringe. I went in to the copy machine in the office, and none of the staff even noticed. I made a copy of the pen lying next to a spoon I had poured salt into to depict my cocaine addiction. When we had to show them as a group, of course my pen was confiscated, and I was told mine was too good. I mean, seriously?

While working on my project in the office, I saw a letter addressed to me on a shelf above the copier from my current boy-friend, who was in prison, Yet another loser, the same one who came to my apartment that night I came so close to OD-ing. I made sure no one was paying attention, grabbed it, and locked myself in the bathroom to read it.

Next thing I knew, they're having a bell ringing downstairs to gather all the women together to discuss some wrongdoing. They noticed immediately that this letter had gone missing and came looking for me. I ripped it into tiny pieces and flushed it, claiming not to know what they were talking about.

Three months or so later, I was granted a pass to go home for a few hours on Christmas to see my kids. I stopped off at the prison as well to visit my loser boyfriend. I should have known the jail kept a record log of visitors and that the halfway house would call and check, knowing I was to have no contact with him.

Long story short, I got kicked out of the halfway house the night before New Year's Eve. One of the biggest triggers and excuse for an addict to party: the holidays! Combine that with the real fear I was going to lose my little girl due to failing to complete the required program. I had every intention of staying clean. I had been clean and sober for about three or four months by that time, had been allowed to go out and find a job while there and was determined to get my life together for my kids. Especially with the threat of losing my baby to her grandparents. I hated them for what they were doing, though now I can actually say we're friends.

Chapter

7

When they told me I had to pack my things and leave immediately, that night, a woman whom I had become friends with there who had come from jail and was on parole begged me to take her with me. I was going to get a motel room right across the street and continue working where I had been till I had money to get an apartment, either in the town I was in or get another job back home.

First big mistake: I let her come along, and it wasn't long after I got a room that she wanted to go get a drink, check out some of the bars in the area. Against my better judgment, my alcoholism won out, and all my good intentions went out the window. It didn't take much for her to twist my arm. Not drinking for so long, my tolerance was way down and I got totally trashed!

By morning, she had convinced me to take her back to her hometown about four hours away. I stopped in to see my boss and tell him what had happened. I assured him I would be back after the New Year in a day or two.

As soon as we reached her hometown, we stopped at a bar where her boyfriend happened to be. He had no idea she was out, so you can imagine how surprised and happy he was to see her. We stayed for a while, drank, and shot some pool. He suggested driving over to some friends of theirs who were having a New Year's Eve party.

The couple whom they were referring to treated me like family, and we spent the night. New Year's Day, still drunk from the night before, we headed back to my hometown. She asked me to stop at another friend's (obviously her sugar daddy), where she scored us a case of beer for the road and some money, and helped herself to a bottle of his Valium.

We were going to stay with a friend of mine and then I was going to get my act together and get my kids back. So I got kicked out of the program. I could still get a job back home. They didn't know I slipped up after leaving. Like I said, still half-lit from the night before, drinking a little hair of the dog while heading back and popping half a Valium was a recipe for disaster.

I got pulled over for my second DUI. about forty-five minutes from our destination. She called her sponsor to come get her because she knew I was being arrested. I wound up as a guest of the Dauphin county prison, and I awoke the next morning, totally disoriented, to a whole new set of problems.

My oldest daughter, Steph, somehow found out where I was, and surprised me with a visit a few days later. I don't think I was ever so happy to see her. She contacted the friend whose house I was heading to that night (my sugar daddy) and talked him into bailing me out. We went to pick up my car, which had been impounded, only to find my so-called friend, after all I had done for her, robbed me blind after they hauled me away! She took my suitcase and travel bag that had been all over Europe with me as a kid.

All my clothes, I later discovered, my most treasured Christmas present from my little girl was gone as well. A beautiful picture Betty gave me of Harley popping out of a huge Christmas box with the lid on her head. I was in tears and absolutely furious! It was the only one they had and was irreplaceable!

The only thing she left me was one of many packs of cigarettes I had just bought and of course what was left of the case of beer, only because she couldn't take that with her. Of course she let the bottle of Valium sit as well, telling the cops it was mine. Lucky for me, they believed me when I told them it was hers, so that was one less charge I was facing. That would've been a much more serious charge than the DUI.

Chapter

8

I met another guy soon after that fiasco while going to score some coke. A really good guy this time, even though he was an addict himself and on parole. He treated me like a princess, and we got along really well. We had so much in common. His sister once said, "No wonder you two get along so good. You're just like him.

When his PO caught up with him, he asked his mom to let me stay with her because I had nowhere to go. He went back upstate to prison, got a year, which turned into two. We would write, and his mom and I would go visit him. One of his sisters was living at home, and she and I became good friends. I referred to her as the sister I never had and his mom as my adopted mom.

His whole family treated me as one of their own. I lived with them for at least a year or so and eventually got my old job back that I had lost a year or two before.

Because of my DUI and being booted out of the halfway house, Harley's grandparents got full custody, which of course gave the addict in me the excuse to keep right on using. They never asked for support, and saw that she still knew her mom. They let her stay over with me because they trusted my boyfriend's mom whom I was living with, and invited me different times to come to their house to spend the night with her. I did once or twice, but I still really resented them for what they had done and stupidly let that get in the way of my spending as much time with Harley as I could have.

I hated the idea of being under their supervision. There were times I never went and didn't even call till a day or two later with some lame excuse. I hate myself when I think back to those times when I'm sure they told her Mommy was coming and I was a no-show. It breaks my heart to think how she was probably all excited and how heartbroken and disappointed she must have been.

Most of the time, I was out getting high and wanted to keep on partying, and I couldn't go out there like that. She's told me since when I told her how sorry I was that it's okay, she forgave me, but I don't know if there will ever come a time that I can forgive myself.

While I was living with my boyfriend's family, I was on probation in two different counties. My no-good ex got out of prison, and I ended up going back with him. I got kicked out of a good home with people who cared and tried to help me out and ended up with really no place to stay again. He ended up on the run from parole when he started using again, and soon after became the biggest coke and crack dealer in town.

The only real reason I stayed with him: I got all my drugs and alcohol for free. We were constantly moving from one place to the next, trying to stay one step ahead of the cops. We'd stay with friends of mine whose houses he was dealing out of or in motel rooms, where the big guns from New York would meet him and drop off five or six ounces of coke and crack at a time. Addicts would trade him guns and knives, even a car once in exchange for the drugs.

He was playing around with a gun one night, aiming it at me, not realizing the safety was off; he almost shot me. Another time, he had me cowering in a corner of a motel room bathroom with a wicked-looking knife, poised to stab me. I thought sure I was dead!

Yet another time I got mouthy with him while high as a kite, and next thing I knew, he had me spread-eagled on the bed. He had my hands cuffed to the bed with handcuffs he had gotten at the adult bookstore and had my ankles tied with electrical cords. He took off, and he and his friend left me there for at least a good two hours, knowing there was an APB out on him. Oh, and did I mention the gag he stuffed in my mouth? There was no way I could get loose. If they had picked him up, I would have died in that room with no one knowing where I was.

When they finally returned, his friend felt sorry for me and got me a drink of water, held it so I could drink. But he wouldn't go against my "boyfriend" and untie me.

Then came the night I OD-ed, for real this time. I had been shooting coke all day. I couldn't get my vein, so he did it for me. He dumped a pile in the spoon, and I told him to take some out, it was too much. Thank God I did. I remember the minute he hit the plunger I was on the bed with no recollection of how I got there, shaking like a leaf. He grabbed me and told me to walk. I couldn't even stand, and all of a sudden, while he's dragging me down the hall, my vision went out, and I was gasping for breath. I remember feeling like a fish out of water and instinctively knew I was about to gasp my last breath, but it was like a dream.

Something inside me clicked and told me, "Candy, what if this isn't a dream? Fight!" About that time, he got me to the bathroom and held me under an ice-cold shower for twenty minutes or I wouldn't be here. There were people partying downstairs, and as I started to come out of it, I heard people talking right there in the room, saying, "What happened?" He told me later there was no one there with us. And at the time I heard this, my vision was still gone, and I remember thinking how nothing had ever looked so black. I said a prayer as he dragged me down the hall, "Please, God, my children need me."

Chapter

9

The next day, the cops busted in downstairs, and hearing the commotion, Rick jumped off the bed where he was bagging up product and headed for the attic, urging me to follow him. I just froze then headed back to the bedroom, locking the door behind me. I was sitting on the edge of the bed while the cops are screaming at me to open the door. They kicked it in and surrounded me with guns drawn, yelling at me to hit the floor. I don't think I was ever so scared, thinking I had just survived an overdose only to be going to jail for who knows how many years and not seeing my kids till they were grown. Harley especially, she was only five or six.

There on the bed sat a mirror with at least an ounce of coke on it, along with packaging material. They had my friend "Mike," the homeowner, and I telling him he was going upstate for ten years and me for at least seven. Talk about being scared. They kept him upstairs while one of them escorted me downstairs, where a bunch of our friends were laughing and joking around with the cops. It was surreal.

Awhile later, the other officers came down, wished us a Merry Christmas, and left—just like that. We were all dumbstruck, like, "What just happened here?" They had told Mike and I we were looking at doing serious time on drug charges, and next thing we know, they're walking out the door! All I can figure is that they knew the drugs were Rick's; he was the one they wanted. Two officers had gone up to search the attic but failed to look in a huge box he was hiding in.

The phone rang about twenty minutes after they left, and it was Rick calling from down the street to see what happened, not expecting anyone to answer. After he heard the cops go downstairs, he said he climbed out the attic window and over onto the neighbor's roof before jumping to the ground and running. He told us where he was, so Mike and I met him there and ended up with him dealing out of yet another place.

Chapter

10

Eventually, the cops caught up with us at a bar. They came in shouting they were looking for Ricky Miller. I was on the pay phone with a friend, trying to score some coke because we were out (that was a first), and because I was with him, they took me along for the ride.

Waking up in the county jail, I was being told they were holding me on yet another DUI I didn't know I had. I had been pulled over while drinking again but never arrested. The results of my blood test had come back, and they didn't know where to find me.

I got out on bail soon after, and Rick went back upstate. So of course I soon hooked up with another man, one whom I met through a friend at work. This was a good man who had gone through rehab and was clean for some time. He had been a pharmacist who got hooked on the prescription meds.

He really loved me and asked me to marry him. He treated my kids really well and stuck by me through a few more of my jail stays. The five years I was with him I spent more time incarcerated than I did with him, but he never gave up on me. He was great and I loved him, but I wasn't in love with him. I ended up cheating on him and really hurting him, something I never meant to do. Staying with him or marrying him wouldn't have been fair to either of us since I didn't feel the same way.

I moved in with "John," this new guy from work. We got an apartment together, and my son Brad moved in with us. By that time, my oldest, Steph, was married and had three kids. I was blessed with three beautiful granddaughters. Aunt Harley was closer in age to her new nieces than she was to her big sister. Sad to say, I was in jail when Steph got married and the first two were born (I missed out on so much due to my addiction and just plain old stupidity).

By the time the youngest was born, I was out and got to be in the delivery room with Steph. Harley had stayed over and gone with us, so that was really exciting for her! John told me he wouldn't get a place with me unless I agreed to marry him. He's been my husband for seventeen years now.

Harley was so excited when I told her Mommy was getting married. She liked John, and I'm sure she saw this as a chance to have two dads since her own dad never really bothered much with her or Macey. About a day or two later, she came over, and it was like a complete turnaround. She pulled me aside and said, "Mommy, don't marry him!" She was really upset, practically begging me, and I didn't know what to think.

I took her to the playground up the street and tried to get her to tell me what had changed from her being so happy and excited just a day or two earlier. She just refused to tell me. All she would say is, "Please, Mommy, don't." She never brought it up again, and everything seemed okay after that.

A few months later, we got married, and she was our ring bearer. She was ten at the time and the only one of my kids who attended my wedding. I don't remember why Steph wasn't there, but Brad refused to be there, saying, "Mom, you haven't known him long enough."

And he was right. Things were okay for a month or two, and all of a sudden, he wasn't the man I thought I had married. He began being downright nasty toward my kids for no reason, Brad who was living with us, as I said, and Harley in particular. All she wanted was for him to like her; she tried so hard, even writing him a really heartfelt letter, and it didn't seem to matter.

We were both still drinking, and I ended up getting another DUI after we had an argument one night, and I took off and went to the bar. John got really nasty and threatened divorce, told me to get a public defender. Even my probation officer looked at him like he couldn't believe it. He just looked at him and said, "Over a DUI, John?"

By that time, I had four DUIs and two drug charges. I'd been in and out of the county jail so many times even I lost count. Most for probation or parole violations. I knew with my record they were bound to throw the book at me, I was terrified they'd send me upstate this time. Up until then, I had always gotten county time and work release.

I got myself a paid attorney who specialized in DUIs. He got me six months in the county with my work release and six months' house arrest upon my release. My son told Harley I was going back to jail before I had a chance to.

I always had a lot of houseplants, and the time before when she knew I was going back, she pulled a leaf off one of my plants and said, "Look, Mommy!" She ripped it in half, saying, "This is my heart when you go to jail."

No child should ever have to say that. Betty tried talking to her about it, and she said, "It's okay, Grandma. I'm used to it."

Chapter

11

As I said, my husband got really nasty, and I was genuinely afraid of losing him. I loved him despite how he was acting. I already had one failed marriage and so many relationships that failed in between, I was determined to make this one work!

I was sitting in jail by that time, and it just hit me that I had finally hit my bottom. I called out to God and prayed like never before. I said, "Lord, I can't do this anymore. I need your help. I need you in my life. Please forgive me."

I started noticing all these little changes, the first being my language. I always had a filthy mouth that just seemed to clean up overnight. I started feeling better about myself and hopeful that with God's help I actually had a shot at a good and normal life. I'd been drinking and using drugs since I was sixteen, and I was now in my early forties. I'd been using most of my life. The only time I had ever been clean was those three or four months in the program.

I started attending church services while doing my time, something I hadn't done since I moved out of my parents' house at eighteen. A different church group came in every week to do a service for us, and there was one I really felt a connection with. Women who didn't even know us genuinely cared.

I went to work one day, and one of my friends informed me that John had been pulled over and arrested for DUI over the weekend.

I went over to his department and asked him if there was something he wanted to tell me. He said, "No." I said, "Seriously? You didn't think I'd find out?"

Once he admitted it was true, things were better than they had been between us in a long time, because now he was going through the same ordeal I was. When I was released in 2001 (my very last prison stay, thank God), he was in rehab and did some jail time of his own after that. We spent our first wedding anniversary at alcohol-safe driving class, of all places. Between the two of us, we had eight DUIs—four each.

I got permission from my probation officer when I got out to go to church on Sundays and attend a Bible study each week. My house arrest monitor only reached so far, so I had to leave at a certain time and be back at a certain time.

There was a woman who came into the prison when I was in to do a Bible study with the inmates every week, and she started a study also for those of us who were out. I attended for about ten years till I started working the night shift and couldn't do it anymore. She and I became good friends, and we still get together once a month to go out to eat.

I started going to the church I had connected with, taking Harley and my granddaughters along. They would spend the weekends with me when I wasn't working. A lot of times Harley attended my Bible study with me as well.

God completely took away my urge for the drugs and alcohol. That's not to say I didn't relapse at all. I did. My cousin whom I had always partied with growing up came home from where he was living out in Colorado. I hadn't seen him in ten long years, and I did drink and do some coke with him for old time's sake, but it didn't have the hold on me it always did before, and when he went back, that was it for me.

I knew how good and amazing God was, and I didn't want that life anymore. I've been clean for about seventeen years now, something I never would have thought myself capable of. But I never could have done it without God's help.

Every time I went to jail, I couldn't wait to get out and get high again. Not so this last time. I had lost out on so much while behind bars. I wanted a better life, not having to be looking over my shoulder all the time and time to spend with my children and grandchildren. And I knew that with God's help was the only way to make that happen. Harley always told me how proud she was of me for cleaning my life up, and that meant so much to me to hear her say that.

I asked the women at church if they still did the prison ministry, and asked if I could be a part of it. They encouraged me to give my testimony, which I did several times, and they were just transfixed; you could have heard a pin drop. It was like they hung on every word. They could relate to me and vice versa because I had been where they were. I told them if anyone had told me even a year ago that I would be going in there, I would have told them they were crazy.

Chapter

12

When I finally got my driver's license back, Harley and I took a mother-daughter camping trip (just the two of us) to the Adirondack Mountains in upstate New York. My parents had been taking me there since I was ten months old, and she was the only one of my kids who had never been there. It was one of my dad's favorite spots; he had been going there since he was a boy.

I had vacation time from work, and we were going for three days, but we ended up staying an extra day. We had an awesome time horseback riding and the one day we spent on the lake in a motorboat we rented. We hit one of the restaurants one night when it rained, and we couldn't use the camp stove. The rest of the time we spent souvenir shopping or just hanging out at the campsite enjoying each other's company.

She had a great time, we both did, and it's one of the memories I'll always cherish. I took my Bible and Daily Bread along, and she'd curl up next to me in her sleeping bag while I read aloud each night. We came home the day before her fourteenth birthday. I have a videotape of our trip together, some that she filmed while I was driving.

About two years after we got married, my husband started acting nasty toward my kids, and for some reason, he was particularly hard on Harley. He was so nice to them when we first got together, and after that, he was like a completely different person around them.

I still think to this day he's always been jealous of my relationship with my kids because his never bother with him. It's sad, but he makes no attempt to reach out to them either. His oldest daughter I have never met to this day, and we've been married for seventeen years. The other three I only met once.

I was finally able to get Harley to open up and tell me why all of a sudden she didn't want me to get married. She said one day when I went to the store and she didn't want to go along that my husband told her flat out, "I don't like you." And when she called Grandma he was constantly in the background telling her to get off the phone.

It breaks my heart to imagine how hurt she had to have felt. I confronted him all this time later, and of course he denied it. He's always had a nasty habit of just coming out with what he thinks, whether it hurts someone's feelings or not. Despite his denial, I don't doubt for a minute that he said just that.

There were times Harley would come over and he wouldn't even so much as say hi until she said hi to him or he'd mutter under his breath, which made both her and I crazy because you just knew it was something nasty. He would always bitch about something when she was here for no reason. She tried so hard with him; all she wanted was for him to like her, and he wouldn't give an inch. Once in a great while he'd be okay, or even halfway civil.

When she was about ten or eleven, she came over one day with a beautiful letter she had written to each of us. This is what she wrote to him, it really tugs on the heartstrings! She was twelve when she wrote these and printed them off her grandparents' computer for us. She was such a loving and caring person.

When she finally confided in me as to what changed her mind about John and me getting married, I asked her why she wouldn't tell me before, and she said, "Because, Mommy, I just wanted you to be happy."

Dear John,

I just wanted to say that I appreciate you for being my stepdad. I know that we don't always get along and that you think that I am a very picky eater and that probably makes you like me less. But that's just the way I am. I will probably change someday, eventually. But until then I hope that you like me just the way I am. I always like you the way you are even when you are in your Grrrrrrrrrring moods! Well we all get like that once in awhile, am I right? HaHa! LOL

Love you Always,
Harley
November 7th, 2002

And mine:

Dear Mom,

I just wanted to say that I appreciate everything that you have ever done for me. Thanx for being there when I needed you and for supplying me with some of the things I need. Thanx for bringing me into the world cause you didn't have to but I'm sure glad you're not one of those women that get abortions. I hope that I am a joy to you cause you sure are a joy to me. Thanx for being my mom and being in my life. You are the best mom a girl could have! There's no other person I would pick to be my mom. I just hope you are happy with your new life with John and as long as you are happy, I'm happy.

And as long as you are sad, I'm sad. You get the picture. Right?

Love You Always,
Harley
November 7th, 2002

She wanted so much to be loved and accepted by him. Betty often tells me that she never really felt like she belonged anywhere. All she wanted when she was little was for her mom and dad to get back together, which is all I wanted for the longest time myself. I guess it just wasn't meant to be. I wish I could have given all my children the wonderful life my parents gave me. If only we had a chance to do things over and get it right.

Betty and Bob gave her a good life and loved her unconditionally. My own mother often said Harley was the lucky one. They always saw that I was a part of her life, something I am so grateful for.

Harley grew up going to church with Betty, as I had always gone with my parents' growing up. In later years, when I accepted Christ and got my life on track, she would go with me. She gave her life to Jesus when she was young. When she was little, she went into Betty and Bob's bedroom dancing around, saying, "Someday, I will. Someday, I will."

They said, "Someday you will what?"

She said, "Someday, I will speak for Jesus!"

Chapter

In 2005, we finally bought a house about a mile from Betty, Bob, and Harley. My husband insisted no one was moving in with us. I couldn't understand how it was his decision alone. It's my house as well as his. All these years I wanted Harley back with me, and I really thought she wanted to move in with us.

Despite what he said she was my daughter, I had lost so many years with her as it was, and we have a three-bedroom. I asked her one day what she thought about moving in with us, and she said, "I don't know, Mom, Grandpa would be so sad." That was all she said, and she never mentioned it again.

I wish I had insisted, but I took that to mean she didn't want to, after all. She did stay over with me a few times and spent a lot of time here. The year after we purchased the house, I had a pool put in, something I had always wanted. I told Harley I did it as much for myself as she and my grandkids.

Two years later, our company shut down, and I was so afraid we'd lose the house. I had been there for twenty-four years and my husband, ten.

I collected unemployment for two years until I finally found a job through a temp agency. It seemed like that's all that was out there. I could get all the overtime I wanted, but we never knew when we were going to get laid off, and trying to pay all the bills was rough at times. My husband had slid into early retirement when his claim ran out and refused to get something part-time, which put a lot of stress on me.

Harley got upset with him one day and told him, "Quit mooching off Mom, and help her with the bills. Be a man!" His retirement was enough to pay the mortgage, but all the other bills added up to more than that, and it was frustrating. But God is good! I was finally able to find this job that paid more than any other temp agency.

Soon after we moved into our new house, Harley got her first job right up the road at a grocery store. I was so proud of her. She really seemed to like it and was working there a year or so.

She told me she had started smoking weed when she was fourteen; she was now sixteen. Here she was with a job she really liked, a perfect attendance record, and just like that, it's gone. She told me they fired her because the register kept coming up short. They thought she was giving too much change. She admitted to me that she was robbing them of hundreds of dollars a day and it was all going up her nose. She had started using coke and crack by then.

Addict that I am (recovering), I can't believe I didn't see the signs, but like every addict, she was a master at hiding it. When she finally told me she was into the coke and crack, she called me one day and said, "Mom, please help me get into a rehab, I need help!"

I picked her up and spent almost the entire day on the phone waiting for one of them to have an available bed, to the point where she was ready to give up. I stressed this to them, and they finally found a facility about forty-five minutes from here. She packed some clothes, and we checked her in.

When Harley said she didn't have cigarettes, the counselor told me I could give her some money to get them there. I was so proud of her admitting to the fact that she needed help. I had never been able to bring myself to do that. The very next morning, she called me, begging me to pick her up. I refused, telling her she was where she needed to be.

A few hours later, I found out she had used the money I had given her for cigarettes and bought a bus ticket home. She, just like me, never liked anyone telling her what to do, and rehabs adhere to strict rules. She said, "Mom, I had to get out of there."

By the time she was seventeen, she was arrested for selling to an undercover officer, not once but twice. Since she had no prior record, and maybe being a minor factored into it, the judge gave her a break. It didn't hurt that she was before the most if not lenient, understanding, and compassionate judge in the county. He and I went way back. He was my public defender for my first drug charge long before he became a judge. As a judge, he is a "fair" man.

He couldn't have gone any easier on her, and I tried stressing to her how lucky she was, that all she had to do was three months' probation. And he even assured her that it would be expunged from her permanent record when she turned eighteen.

Chapter

14

From that moment in time, her life just started to spiral out of control. I don't think she even made it a month before her probation officer got her for a "hot urine." She gave her a chance, kept asking Harley if it was going to be clean, and Harley insisted up and down it would, that she wasn't doing any drugs. A few minutes later, the officer came back into the room and told us it was hot for opioids. Harley told me it was coke until I told her that wouldn't show up as an opioid, coke is a stimulant. She then admitted she had been taking morphine pills. Needless to say, she had violated her probation and was now looking at jail time—her first of many in the county prison.

I had taken Harley with me and my prison ministry group into the county prison a year or two before so she could get a sense of what it was like. My intention was to try to impress on her that she didn't ever want to end up in there herself. It seemed as if she connected with the inmates in that short hour and wasn't at all intimidated. The exact opposite effect I had hoped for. Looking back on it now, I think maybe she knew someone in there and they told her it wasn't so bad.

The judge had sentenced her to three months, five years, meaning if she didn't make it the three months she would end up in jail for those three months and have to do the remaining time up to the five years on probation or parole. She wasn't in long, but it didn't seem to faze her. Like me, she got out and went right back to using and dealing, hanging out with the same crowd. She would call me all the time, wanting rides here and there, usually into town, where she got into trouble.

I soon realized I wasn't helping her by doing so, and I finally put my foot down, telling her I wasn't going to continue to enable her. I told her there would be no more rides into town. If she needed a ride home, I would pick her up, but I would not take her, and I refused to give her any more money. If she needed something, I would take her to get it or pick it up for her, but I would not hand her cash like I had in the past. Her grandpa eventually did the same.

Like any addict, she was a master manipulator and had Grandpa wrapped around her little finger. He started buying her cigarettes and phone cards instead of giving her money.

Chapter

15

Around 2010, she was seeing a guy who was into the drugs as much as she, and he was on the run. She would go with him wherever he went. I knew he had a gun and that in itself scared me. I was so afraid she'd end up getting shot. Eventually the police caught up with him, and he went to jail.

It wasn't long before she was with someone else, a guy who was pretty heavy into dealing coke and crack. This guy had even done time on Riker's Island in NYC on drug charges. The apartment he was living in was the same place I used to go to for my drugs when she was little. She had been there with me all those years ago.

She was partying with and was in jail with quite a few of the same women who were in with me. One day, I said to her, "Honey, these are people I used to party with back in the day, and they're still out there getting high and in and out of jail. Do you want that to be you when you get to be as old as they are?"

"Doesn't that tell you something?"

When it comes to drugs in this town, everyone knows everyone.

She, like me, was in and out of jail so many times I've even lost count, and I think she probably did too. For both of us, the majority of the time we spent in there was for probation or parole violations. Only Harley did some state time. Between those three to five years she originally got, she got sentenced to a women's prison about an hour and a half away. She did about two and a half years the first time, some of it there and some at the other end of the state, a six-hour drive, one way.

She ended up going back later on and maxed out, served the remainder of her time. I was so proud of her. She got her GED while she was up there. She was the only one of my three kids to graduate and receive her diploma. One of my biggest regrets is that I wasn't there for her graduation. I was working for the temp agency at the time, and we didn't get any personal days or anything. I wish every day I had just called in sick and been there for her. She said it was no big deal because she was in jail, and I said, "No, honey. It was a very big deal, a real accomplishment, and I'm so sorry I wasn't there for it."

Chapter

16

In 2011, I got a call at work from my baby. She wouldn't say what was wrong, but it was obvious she was freaking out. She wanted me to meet her when I got off that night and asked me if I had a clean pair of underwear in my truck. She was beside herself, and as soon as I got there, I asked her if she had been raped. She said, "Yes."

A guy whom she thought was her friend whose apartment she was at raped her, holding a knife to her throat. Her own knife she carried for protection with a wicked blade. We were sitting in my truck, and she kept telling me to keep my voice down, that he was somewhere behind us listening.

I wanted to get her out of there, take her home, but she refused to go anywhere because her stash of drugs was in his place and she needed to sell it. I knew if I just drove off with her the minute I stopped for a traffic light she would have taken off and gone back anyway. When she did get out of there, I told her she needed to press charges, she couldn't let him get away with it.

Her grandpa took her to the police station, and they actually had the audacity to say they didn't believe her! Bob pointed out that the locations of the marks on her couldn't have possibly been done by herself, which is what they were implying. So the bastard is still out there, free to do it again.

My heart went out to her. First to be violently raped at knifepoint and then to more or less be called a liar by our police force who have sworn to protect in cases like this really devastated her emotionally and just reinforced her distrust of authority figures. I can't begin to imagine her fear, pain, and sense of hopelessness.

In 2012, she met and fell in love with a guy whom she was planning a future with. He convinced her to turn herself in so she could get all these charges behind her and have a clean slate so they could get married when she got out. She really loved and trusted him, and once she was back behind bars, he pretty much turned his back on her! She cried to me that he wasn't answering her letters to him and she was going crazy wondering what was going on. I went to his house quite a few times, and he acted like he didn't want to come to the door.

Next thing I knew, she told me she found out he had slept with Macey, her sister, soon after she turned herself in. She was devastated! She was in tears, saying, "Mom, why is it every time I give my heart to a man, they stomp on it?" I felt so bad for her and wished there were something I could do to make it all better.

This same year, she was going to stay overnight with a friend and just got a bad feeling. She called Grandpa to pick her up and found out the next morning her friend's house where she was supposed to stay at burned down and he died in the fire. He had been drinking, had left the stove on, and had fallen asleep. If she had stayed, she would have died then too.

It wasn't until years later when I ran into one of my best friends that she told me she had left or divorced her husband because all he wanted to do was party. He was the friend whom Harley was talking about. I never knew it was him at the time or that Harley had even known him.

Chapter

17

When she got out after that, she got into doing the bath salts. Macey had been arrested along with a bath-salts ring in town, and when she was pulled over, she told them her name was Harley, and they actually charged Harley with it until Macey finally owned up to it and recanted her statement. Harley was understandably furious with her, and they were on the outs with each other for a long time. They were locked up in the county at the same time quite a few times.

One night, Harley was doing bath salts with a friend in a known crack house in town when this so-called friend literally tried pushing her out the second-story window of his room! There's a sidewalk directly below and, when she showed me where it happened, I could see that the glass pane was cracked and broken. Thank God she hung on to that frame with every ounce of strength she had, or she most likely would have died or ended up a paraplegic!

Another night, high on salts again, she called Grandpa to pick her up in town, insisting that someone was after her and trying to kill her. He told her to go across the street and wait for him. When he got there, she was nowhere around. She would do that a lot when high on salts, ask us to come pick her up and she wouldn't be where she said she'd be. He drove around and finally went back home, worried but not knowing what else to do.

She had walked up the block to the YMCA and asked to use their phone. Someone in there saw how high she was and called the police. They called Bob and told him she was on her way back to jail. I had called him to see if he had heard from her because I had gotten a really bad feeling that something was wrong, and that's when he told me what happened.

When she didn't go back on probation violations, she always ended up back in there for being on the run from her PO. They would always approve her home plan to her grandpa's, meaning they had to know she would be staying with him before they released her. She would get out and go back to using every time, and then knew if they came to check on her she'd be hot with the drugs in her system and she'd go right back in. So she would hang with people in town and be on the run all over again.

What I don't understand is why they kept approving her home plan for out there, knowing it never worked. A lot of times she would go out there in the wee hours, knowing they wouldn't be looking for her then. She would stay over and leave the next day.

One night, she had done that, and five police cars pulled into the driveway the next morning (you'd think she was one of America's most wanted), and she saw them. She ran out the back door and into the woods and hid out there until they left.

Another time she was there, her probation officer showed up, looked into the window, and saw her. She said he yelled in, "Harley, I know you're in there, open the door!" They told Bob later if she hadn't they would have broken it down.

There were times her grandpa would cover for her and tell them she wasn't there when she was sleeping. He didn't want her going back to jail. None of us wanted to see her keep going back, but at the same time, I felt she was safer in there and I didn't have to worry so much. I felt bad for him; he just wanted her home, but she never stayed.

I know she wanted to do right and have a normal life, she just didn't know how. She had been into the drugs for so long she didn't know any other way. There really wasn't anyone her age out there, and she liked being in town where the action was. She got bored out there, and that's a big trigger for an addict.

As far as the home plan, the system failed her over and over again. They court ordered her to rehab once, and she had her so-called friend pick her up. They knew she was an addict and needed help. Instead of releasing her over and over, they should have kept putting her in rehab. What they need are rehabs where they can't just walk off. They need to start having locked facilities.

Chapter

18

One night in 2012, I got a call from Harley around midnight. I was in bed but still awake. She was all worked up, wanting me to come get her, saying some guy was chasing her. She ran down the street and pounded on an elderly woman's door, begging her to let her in. She said it seemed like she wasn't going to, but it was the dead of winter with snow on the ground, and she said she thought she took pity on her when she saw Harley was barefoot.

She said she wanted me to take her out to Grandpa's, but when I got there, Harley changed her mind and wanted me to drop her off at a friend's on the other side of town. She was really nervous, saying this guy was looking for her.

When I asked her what was going on, she said she had been at his house partying with him and, when he had gone to the bathroom, she grabbed the five ounces of crack he had sitting there and took off. She said she didn't have time to put her shoes on, she heard him coming out of the bathroom and ran! I was, like, "You've got to be kidding me, you're telling me you've got five ounces of crack in my truck?"

At that hour, we passed quite a few cops, and I said to her later if we had been pulled over for anything, with my record (clean all these years or not), they would have locked me up right along with her.

I told her she was playing a dangerous game. People get killed over drugs all the time for a lot less than what she stole from him.

She got on the phone and called ahead to whoever she was going to see and bragged about how she was running this town and how they were going to party when she got there. There was a crowd on the sidewalk when I pulled up, and some young guy came right over, lifted her out of the truck, and carried her because she had no shoes.

As it turned out, the building she went into was the same apartment building her dad had been living in when I first met him. For all I know, it might have been the same apartment.

As I said, she maxed out upstate, meaning she was free and clear of probation and parole. She had a clean slate to start over and have a good life, free of the drugs and destruction that go hand in hand with that lifestyle. I kept telling her she couldn't go back to the same people, whether she considered them her friends or not. That's the first thing they tell you in rehab: you can't go back to the same people, places, or things and expect to stay clean.

I would try my best to encourage her, tell her not to put herself in a situation where she knew people were using, not to put herself in temptation's way. But she loved being around people, meaning hanging in town. She was way too trusting, believing everyone to be her friend. She had such a huge heart. She would have done anything for anyone and wanted to believe the best in everyone she met.

Chapter

In 2013, she reconnected with a guy whom she had always had a big crush on in high school, and they finally got together. This man was without a doubt the love of her life. She told me she had loved him forever and now he was finally hers.

When I met him, they were living in a trailer in a local campground. I picked her up one day, and we went shopping and out to lunch. She told me she would have to call and check on him. She was worried about him because he was shooting heroin, that he was a longtime addict. She admitted to me that she had tried it and was doing it too, but she said, "Mom, I'm not shooting up, I'm just snorting it. If I ever start shooting up, I swear I'll kill myself."

Around Christmas, she called me, wanted me to take her to the emergency room. She was so sick and in so much pain that Nate carried her out to my truck. It turned out she had pneumonia and needed antibiotics. She had no health insurance and no way to pay for them.

The doctor was really concerned when he heard this, and awhile later, he came back into her room and told her he had gone down to the pharmacy in the hospital and paid for her medication himself. He told her to consider it a Christmas gift. Talk about an act of compassion.

I said to her, "You know that was God at work, don't you?"

A few weeks later, she told me she had started shooting up the heroin. She came up to my mom's for Christmas with us, had her friend bring her after she ate out at Grandma and Grandpa's. By that time, she was on the run again, said she was driving and had passed a cop. She said, "Mom, he stared right at me. I know he knew it was me. I whipped around the corner and into a parking lot, told Tim to pop the trunk. I rode the rest of the way up here in the trunk while he drove."

She said she almost didn't make it, thought sure she was going back to jail. Little did any of us know that would be her last Christmas with us and the first time in twenty years she got to talk to my uncle all the way from Maine. She had pulled up in the driveway right after he called. None of us had seen or heard from him in those twenty years until my mom finally tracked him down. He and his wife, Shelly, had taken Harley overnight when I was moving. They were a loving Christian couple who couldn't have children of their own, and they were thrilled to spend time with her. My aunt Shelly died not all that long after that. My uncle sold the house and seemingly disappeared off the face of the earth.

Harley and Nate had become engaged, but both were so far into their heroin addiction that they started breaking into convenience stores to support their habit. They would have Tim, always the enabler, drive them. The police and probation officer caught up with Nate, and the judge granted him rehab, Teen Challenge, a Christian program instead of jail time. The judge told him it was his last chance and against his better judgment.

Nate eventually got a day pass to come home and asked Harley to get him some heroin. She blamed herself for not telling him no. She told me he had died in her arms but she got him to the hospital and they were able to save him with the Narcan. From then on, they were on the run again because he knew he was going to jail if he went back.

They somehow connected him with the convenience store robberies and questioned Harley quite a few times as well. Nate took the fall for all of them because he wanted to protect Harley. All they had of Tim was his car on camera, and they couldn't make out the make and model. The love of her life got five to ten years upstate. I believe he still has a year or two to do.

Harley was absolutely devastated. She was so in love with this man, and Tim did everything he could to try to break them up. She was determined to wait for him and planned on marrying him when he got out. She went through a deep depression and felt so alone knowing it would be years until she could be with him again.

After he went upstate, her life spun out of control all over again. For a while, he wasn't answering any of her letters. She felt so lost without him, and not hearing from him made it all the worse for her. She never gave up on him or on their plans for their future together despite Tim's efforts to come between them. She was head over heels in love with this man. She told me she met this Tim through her sister Macey. She was supposedly engaged to him, but once Macey got out of jail, she kicked him to the curb.

Chapter

20

In May of 2015, I got laid off from the plant I had been working at but placed in another location with the same company. This place only needed us a few days a week. On a Thursday, I was told if they needed me the next day I would get a call in the morning. They always called at exactly 7:00 a.m., if that was the case.

That next morning, at exactly 7:00 a.m., I was awakened by the phone, thinking, "Well, it looks like I'm working today, after all." It wasn't my job at all. It was Betty telling me Harley had OD-ed, that she was on her way to the hospital. That was all she said before hanging up, so I had no idea how bad it was. I jumped out of bed and into my clothes and rushed to the hospital.

When I got there, Harley was in the emergency room waiting to be released. Her grandpa Bob always goes to yard sales and auctions in the wee hours of the morning. That particular day, he said something told him not to go. He said that never happens, but he went back to sleep.

He got up at about 6:00 a.m. and went to the bathroom. Harley had stayed over and was sleeping in his and Betty's old room, that in order to get to it you had to go through the bathroom. He heard what he later realized was her gulping her last breath and went in to see what it was. He said she wasn't breathing and had no pulse. He attempted CPR, which he had never done, and was able to get her breathing again until the paramedics got there with the Narcan to reverse the effects of the heroin.

I could tell she was just itching to get out of there and didn't seem to comprehend the seriousness of what had just happened. She was actually dead when Bob found her! I motioned Betty aside and told her if she didn't call Harley's probation officer I would. In an overdose case, the hospital is required to contact the police, something obviously no one had done.

I said to Betty, "There's no way we can let her go back out there. I can tell she's just itching to get high again."

Betty agreed and called the probation office, who took their sweet time getting there. We asked the hospital staff to stall till they got there. They told Harley she couldn't leave until they got certain test results back. She had just gone down the hall to the bathroom when they finally showed up. They wouldn't even let us stay to say good-bye to her, saying she was now in custody. After we had been the ones to call them, that didn't sit too well with me. Seeing how determined she was to go back out there, much as I didn't want to see her back in jail, I felt she was safer in there.

While she was in, I got permission from Betty to search her room from top to bottom. Being an addict myself, I knew to check places most people wouldn't even think to look. I found a syringe or two and a few empty bags, but nothing more. I thought sure she had more stashed somewhere, but I failed to find it. If there was more, I didn't want her getting her hands on it when she got out.

She got out a few weeks later, and sure enough, she had more from the same deadly batch. When she had first told me she was using heroin, I begged her to stay away from the stuff, telling her it was all over the news that it was being cut with fentanyl, something more deadly than the heroin itself.

I was incredulous when she told me she'd never get any of that, that she only got it from certain people she trusted. "They wouldn't do that, Mom," she said.

I said, "But, honey, you don't know who they get it from and who they get it from!"

The bags she got that she had OD-ed on, she said she didn't get at the usual place. When she got out, she was at a friend's babysitting, and the kids wanted to go to the park. She told the little girl they could go but to be back in a half hour. Their dad was at work about forty-five minutes away, and she said he told her later he got this very strong feeling that something was horribly wrong at home and he had to get back immediately. He told her he was driving the whole way doing ninety miles an hour, driving over lawns and running traffic lights to get there.

As soon as he walked in the door, his ten-year-old daughter said, "Daddy, Harley's sleeping on the bathroom floor, and I can't wake her up."

He said she was blue when he found her. He rushed her to the paramedics station in the small town they lived in, and at first, they acted like they didn't want to help her because they were the same ones to respond to Bob's 911 call just a week or two earlier. She said one of the paramedics told her she didn't realize how lucky she was that his partner wanted to try a third time with the Narcan or she wouldn't have made it; she was that far gone.

He told her they are only supposed to give two shots of the stuff. I told her once again she had to see that that was divine intervention in both those cases.

She said, "I know, Mom. God's not going to save me a third time."

When I told her I had searched her room and asked her where she had it, she said it was inside her phone (goes to show you how ingenious addicts are when it comes to hiding their stash), but Betty said it couldn't have been because she had Harley's phone. Harley said it was from the same batch as before, but she said she thought having it sit all that time while she was locked up that it would have diluted somewhat or lost some of its potency, but she said obviously it hadn't.

The way she talked when she told me about it, I still don't think she grasped the enormity of it. She didn't know how long she was without oxygen to her brain this last time, but she said since then there was a lot she couldn't remember because of it. As it turns out, God did save her a third time she OD-ed, and they had to administer the Narcon three times that same month.

Chapter

21

In the months ahead, she was back to being in and out of jail countless times on shoplifting charges and probation violations due to the new charges. Her fines Bob was paying on for her just kept racking up. He told me one day that over the years they had totaled up to approximately $32,000. I don't know how they can expect anyone to pay that.

That same year, 2015, I finally got hired on with the company I had been working for through the temp agency for the last six years. The Lord has truly blessed me with a good-paying job. In the beginning, we were working seven days a week. I was second shift at the time, so I had some time to spend with Harley before or after work, but I had no days off.

A few months later, our department went to twelve-hour shifts, where we work four and five day weeks and then have four and five days off unless we sign up for overtime. Or they can force us in but no more than two of our days off. I am so thankful we went to the twelve hours when we did because that allowed Harley and I lots of time to spend together. We went out to eat and shopped a lot, or she would come over here to swim or just hang out.

She ended up doing time in the county prison again and was in, in July of 2015. On July 22, I was in the breakroom waiting to punch out and go home when I saw I had a text from my oldest daughter,

Steph. She told me she had seen on Betty's Facebook that her grand-daughter Macey had been found dead of a heroin overdose that day.

I couldn't believe it. I was in shock when I read it, thinking it had to be a mistake. I had a message from Betty too, telling me there was a death in the family, to call her. While I was at work earlier, not knowing a thing about it, Betty had gotten permission to go in to the prison to tell Harley before someone else did. She had to tell her through the glass in the visiting room, not even being able to hug her.

I thank God for my good friend Marilyn, who is the prison chaplain. She went in with Harley, so she wasn't alone when she got blindsided with this horrible news. Poor Betty had to go in by herself too as they would only allow one family member in to deliver the news. I can only imagine how extremely hard it was on both of them. Harley and Macey had just before that gotten to a good place in restoring their relationship. I know Harley was very thankful for that.

I couldn't help thinking it was a good thing Harley was in there when it happened, or she could have very well ended up dead herself trying to numb the pain if she had been out. Still, my heart broke for her as well as her dad and grandparents, and especially her mom.

Macey was only twenty-four, and a real sweetheart. It's been two years now that she's been gone, and there was never any justice. They know she was dumped on a filthy mattress in a garage in town, but they've never been able to find out who dumped her there.

One day, not all that long before she died, I had been dropping a friend off after church, and I heard someone calling my name. It was Macey. She came running across the street with a friend and asked me if I could give them a ride. They hopped in, and when I dropped them off, she gave me a big hug and said, "Love you, Candy." That was the last time I saw her.

I knew through Harley that Macey was into the drug scene too and doing heroin as well, but it still came as an awful shock to every-one. Betty told me she was really worried about "Jim," her son, and Harley and Macey's dad. He was really taking it hard.

A week or so later, Macey's mom had a memorial service for her. Marilyn, the prison chaplain who had been with Harley when she received the devastating news, arranged it that Harley could get a furlough. Bob was able to pick her up at the prison about a half hour before the service and had to have her back at a certain time.

I pulled into the parking lot, and they were already there. She was pacing on the lot, talking on Tim's phone, and I had a feeling of dread, knowing she was up to something. I gave her a big hug, and she took the vase of hot pink roses I had ordered for the family from Harley, Steph, and Brad and I. Harley assured me Macey would have loved them.

The phone call minutes before really worried me, because Tim would take her wherever she wanted to go at any time and even buy her the drugs. This day in particular had to be the ultimate trigger for her. Every time I lit into Tim about taking her for the drugs, he would say, "I just can't say no to her." He was a very big part of the problem because he was constantly enabling her.

I kept telling her she needed to get him out of her life, but he was her ride everywhere and her sugar daddy. She would often say, "Mom, I can't stand him," but she was always with him because of the drugs. He was an addict's dream come true. He had to know she was using him, but he was always there anyway.

I think he did love her in his own warped way, but he was absolutely no good for her, and we kept praying he would leave her alone. He had been obsessed with Macey, and when she died, he turned his obsession on my daughter despite her telling him from day 1 that they would never be anything but friends. I told him one day that he needed to leave her alone and find someone his own age.

Tina, Macey's mom, was standing outside as we went to go in, and she wrapped her arms around Harley, tears streaming down her cheeks, and said, "Harley, I'm begging you. Please stop this before you end up like Macey."

Harley had been outside during the service smoking a cigarette and came in about a half hour later, claiming she was hungry and was going across the street with Tim to get something to eat at Hardee's. We all looked at her and said, "No!" Bob reminded her he had just stopped at McDonald's on the way and had gotten her something. He said, "You can't be hungry."

Of course, Harley, being Harley, insisted until he told her to go ahead but to make sure she came right back because they had to leave to have her back at the prison in about fifteen minutes. I couldn't help thinking she could have asked Tim to run with her and he would have done it.

I knew deep down she wasn't going to get something to eat; she was going to meet someone there to get heroin. I figured from the start that that's what the phone call had been about when I got there. She did come back a few minutes later, gave everyone a hug, and she and grandpa headed out. I found out later that she did indeed score some heroin and shot up in the restaurant's bathroom before coming back.

I don't know if the prison personnel could tell that she was high or just did a routine drug test on her when she went back. But she got busted and got sent to the hole (solitary confinement) for thirty days. In there, they take certain privileges away. For those thirty days, when we would visit her, she would come into the visiting room in a bright red jumpsuit as opposed to the customary drab green, and had pink handcuffs on, which was a little ridiculous, considering she was behind the glass. They would also have leg shackles on her. I don't know what the point of that was.

I hated to see her on the run and back in jail all the time, but at the same time, I would breathe a sigh of relief, feeling that she was safer in there. I know there are just as many if not more drugs in there as there are on the street, but at least in there, there would always be someone with her if, heaven forbid, something would happen.

One day, when the prison had her housed on the work-release block because of overcrowding, she called Grandpa and told him, "They have snack machines over here. If you put money on my account [which we always did so she could get the necessities she needed], they'll take half of it. Could you please meet of friend of mine in here at her job and give her twenty dollars for me? That way, I'll get to keep the whole amount."

Believing her story, he did. I knew from all the time I spent on the work-release side that the women just being housed there and not eligible to go out to work had to work in the prison to get their money for the machines. The others had to do without any cash on hand. He didn't know that and believed every word she said. I saw right through it when he told me and knew she was either going to buy drugs in there with it or have her "friend" bring the drugs in to her. There was no sense in telling him that because it wouldn't have done any good. Naturally, she got a random drug test that time too and spent her first stay in the hole.

Chapter

22

There was a young man at work three years younger than Harley whom I had worked with as a temp. He got hired on with the company before I did. I didn't really know him at the time, and there were rumors at work that he was into drugs and there was no way he would pass the drug test required for hiring.

I got to talking to him in the breakroom one night, and he told me he had been into drugs and turned his life around. He was going to church, and had even started a recovery group he referred to as RTC—Recovery through Christ. He, Tyler, told me he was using his tablet on his breaks to write to inmates to encourage them to get on the right path.

I told him about my daughter, her being in jail again, and asked him if he would be willing to write to her. He wrote her a letter almost right away, and they were writing back and forth the rest of the time she was in there. I felt that he was a really good influence on her and being so close to her age and hearing his story she could relate better to him. He wrote her faithfully, and she would always write him back.

Then came the day that she got out, and I thought she would be interested in meeting him. Instead, she more or less blew him off, saying, "Mom, I think Grandma would get along better with him than I would. All he talks about is God."

I said, "Harley, he spent all that time writing to you, a lot of the time on his breaks at work. I thought you would want to meet him."

One day, my son and I had taken her to Longhorn Steak House. I didn't want her to be out there using, knowing it was the year anniversary of Macey's death, and she loved going there. She had been wanting to go again, and we planned to go on my next day off on the weekend.

I mentioned it to Tyler the night before and, said he was welcome to join us. He gave me the impression that he had other plans and probably wouldn't. I got a text from him the next morning, saying, "I'm coming, I'll be there."

Harley wanted to bring along one of her guy friends, and I told her I would rather it just be her and I because I had a surprise for her. She had never seen any pictures of him, but from the way I described him to her, she knew who he was the minute we walked in. He got there first and had been saving a booth for us.

I'll never forget her reaction. She went running over to him, yelling, "Tyler!", threw her arms around him, and gave him a hug. She slid into the booth beside him as if she had known him all her life. She seemed so happy to have finally met him and told me later how she had texted Grandma under the table, saying, "Mom had the best surprise for me."

She said, "Oh my gosh, Mom, he's gorgeous. He smiled, and I just melted!"

They really hit it off, and I was so happy for her, she really liked him. From then on, he would pick her up after work in the morning and take her out for coffee or breakfast. She always looked forward to that. The first time he picked her up, she told me afterward that they had gone to a local park and just sat and talked for hours. She said, "Mom, I had such a good time. We talked about God and everything we could think of."

She always looked forward to seeing him. I asked her one time if he ever kissed her or made a move on her. She looked at me like I was crazy and said, "No. Do you really think I could keep something like that to myself if he had?" Of course she told him I had asked her that. She was always very outspoken. She was fun loving and so full of life, loyal to a fault, especially to her family.

Granted, she had a lot of deep-seated resentments toward her dad and I, understandably for not being there for her so many times when she was growing up. She had every right to feel that way, and I would give anything to be able to go back. There are so many things I wish I had done differently, so, so many if-onlys. We were finally getting to a really good place in our mother-daughter relationship, and she told me she had forgiven me for all the times I wasn't there.

"It is what it is, Mom," she'd say.

Chapter

23

The last time the law caught up with Harley was on September 2016. She had only been out two months this time. Because of a shoplifting charge in another county, they extradited her to their prison—not all that far away, thankfully. The short time she was there, I only had one visit with her.

When she was locked up, she would say jail was her safe place. I could tell her attitude hadn't changed at all, that it would be the same old, same old if they released her. She told me that they were going to bring her back to our county prison where she had always done her time, with the exception of the years she spent in state prison. She said she was looking at doing about sixteen months back home here, and asked me to send her some books and a nice journal once they had transferred her.

She loved to read and wrote beautiful poetry. She said writing poems was her way to vent. A lot of her poems were about her addiction, and they portrayed how much pain she was in, the shame and utter hopelessness of this disease. A lot of them were about God and her desire to get out of this destructive lifestyle she was leading. Reading them breaks my heart all over again.

In the meantime, Bob found out he might be able to bail her out with only $100. I never heard of anyone's bail ever being that low. Betty left a message on my phone, saying Bob wanted to know if I could help him with the money. I called him and left a message of my own, saying that I couldn't in all good conscience do that. I told him I could just give him the money, but I wasn't going to be a part of it because I would never be able to forgive myself if I helped bail her out and she ended up like Macey.

The very next day, October 8, 2016, Harley called me, all excited, saying, "Mom, I'm out." I was happy for her, but had a feeling of dread. I knew she wasn't ready. I also knew she had a court hearing in two days and told her I had the day off, that I wanted to go with her. She told me she had no intention of going.

I said, "What? You mean to tell me you're going to be on the run again already? Why would you do that?"

She told me the probation office dropped the ball. They were supposed to have a detainer on her when she got back here to prevent her from getting bail and that they had failed to do that. She said if she went to court they would realize they screwed up royally and she would be right back in.

As always, she knew they would be looking for her at Grandpa's, so she had been staying with a guy whom she met through her sister Macey. He had been arrested as part of the same bath-salts ring Macey had and was also on the run. He was now into meth, and Harley and he were constantly fighting because he told her he didn't want her doing the heroin because he had lost too many friends to heroin deaths. She would disappear on him all the time to get it anyway, and he was getting fed up.

But I'm getting ahead of myself. Back in July of that same year, when she had been released from the county is when she started hanging out with this man. My mom and I were grocery shopping in a town up the road from ours when Harley called me. She was literally freaking out, saying, "Mom, please come get me. Grandpa and I just had a big fight, and he's driving me crazy. I have to get out of here. He knows I'm high on meth, you gotta pick me up."

I told her she would have to wait awhile, that I was at the store with my mom. I was ready to go but was out in the car waiting for her to come out of the store. I told her I would call her when I was on my way out to Bob's. I said, "I can't just leave your grandma in the store and take off without her."

When I did pick her up, I told her she couldn't come to my place acting all high because my mom was there. Instead of going right home, she had decided to stay and swim with us. She's said many times she's so glad she stayed that day because as it turned out that's the last time she saw her youngest granddaughter.

Around that same time, Harley and my oldest granddaughter (her niece) and I went out for lunch at Olive Garden and some shopping afterward. We had a good time, and I was so glad Taylor (my granddaughter) was off from work that day and could go with us. My oldest, Steph, had kept Harley from seeing the girls for years because of her being into the drugs. Harley told me one day that Steph had called her out of the blue and wanted her to come over. She later told me Steph was shooting heroin too. I had no idea.

Of course when I confronted her about it, she denied it up and down. My son-in-law left her, and she hooked up with a guy whom Harley got her heroin from. But that's a story for another time.

Suffice it to say, they (both Steph and this Josh) are both in jail, Steph waiting to go to rehab any day now. Please keep her in your prayers. I cannot lose another child.

Chapter

24

Getting back to Harley, she and I would text back and forth or talk on my breaks the days I worked. I would get up to go in at night, and I'd text her, "Good morning, baby, I'm up."

We made a game of what she'd always say when she was little. She would usually get right back to me, telling me she loved and missed me or making plans to do something together on my next day off. She sent me a text one night in December, saying, "Mom, you're going to love what I got you for Christmas! Can you meet me at my friend's when you get off in the morning? I'm afraid if I don't give it to you early I'm going to lose or break it."

At 3:00 or 4:00 a.m., I talked to her, told her I would call or text her as I was leaving work at 6:30 a.m. so she would know to look for me. Until then, I didn't know where she was staying, and it would be hard to see the house number in the dark.

When I left work, I texted her and tried calling but got no response. I assumed she had probably fallen asleep and left another message for her, saying I was getting close to home and if I didn't hear from her soon I was going home to bed because I had to work again that same night.

When I got up, my husband told me Harley had stopped over and asked him to wake me up so she could give me my Christmas present. He said he didn't want to do that because I had to work, so she left my present with him. I told her she was right, I absolutely love it and I would cherish it always. It's a beautiful black-and-white heart-shaped diamond necklace. It's the first and only Christmas present she ever got me on her own, which makes it all the more special.

We had the same idea: jewelry, hearts, and diamonds. I had bought her a blue-and-white heart-shaped diamond ring that would have matched her beautiful blue eyes. She never got to see it or to see me wear her necklace.

Chapter

25

She and I had gone for tacos and to the mall about a week before to get Taylor's Christmas present. She was saying how she wanted *sooo* bad to get off the heroin and she needed money to get suboxone, a drug that when taken if she would do heroin would put her in immediate withdrawal and make her sick. Clinics use this drug kind of like the methadone to wean addicts off the heroin.

Being on the run, she couldn't go to a clinic, and she had no health insurance. She said she had a friend she could get some from. That she really wanted off it now but didn't want to go to rehab yet because she wanted to be home for Christmas. I told her I wanted more than anything to see her off it too and I hoped she really meant it.

I believe this drug is also known to reduce the cravings for the heroin. Steph had a prescription for it years ago from her doctor when he became addicted to Vicodin and kept telling Harley she needed to get suboxone. Harley kept saying she wanted to get into rehab but kept putting it off because she didn't want to go back to jail until they had a bed for her in rehab, which, being on the run, is what she would have had to do.

Betty said she thinks she was afraid one of us would die while she was in jail. We tried getting her into a mental health facility, but they wouldn't take her because she was on drugs. I kept asking her what it was going to take, considering she had lost at least six friends to heroin, along with her own sister.

"I'm terrified the same things are going to happen to you if you don't stop this," I would tell her.

When asked what it was going to take, she replied, "I don't know, Mom."

I prayed every day for God to keep his wall of protection around her at all times, to protect her from the drugs and from herself as well as knocking some sense into her. He had been so faithful in keeping her safe. Each time she OD-ed and actually died, God put someone in her life to save her. I was so sure God was keeping her alive for a reason; she would have had one heck of a testimony for others. I had such faith that she would eventually get it right and have a long happy, healthy life ahead of her, free of this horrible addiction.

I told her I would give her the money for the suboxone as long as it went for that (she called her friend while with me and asked him to get it for her). It was supposed to be enough to last her two weeks. In exchange, I asked her to promise me she would go to Tyler's church with me that Sunday, two days away. He had been trying to get her to go to his RTC group as well but so far hadn't succeeded. She had promised to go to my church with me twice before, but she would walk out almost as soon as she got there, so I was really hoping she would, but I wasn't holding my breath.

The next day, after getting the suboxone, she seemed really good. I could tell she definitely wasn't high, and she seemed happy. I was really glad I had given her the money, and it seemed like this was going to work. I was really leery of giving it to her, praying it wasn't going for heroin, but I really couldn't *not* give it to her, considering she seemed so sincere and called the friend with me right there. With her so obviously being drug-free the next day, I felt sure I had done the right thing and she would be okay.

The following day, Sunday, December 4, she did come over to my house that morning to go to church with me. Betty came as well, anxious to meet Tyler, who seemed to be having such a positive influence on her. It was 7:30 a.m. when Harley arrived, saying she had to quickly go to the bathroom before we left.

Betty and I exchanged a look, both of us knowing without a shadow of a doubt that Harley was high as a kite. But she was there and going with us, that was the important thing. Considering, I was amazed she showed up at all. I had wanted her to stay overnight with me so she was there, but at the last minute, she said she was staying with this friend who was also on the run because she wanted him to go along.

He brought her over and was sitting out front waiting for us, and all of a sudden, I saw him drive off. To this day, I don't know why he left, and I have never met him. Instead, we got to the church, and Tim showed up, the last person I wanted to see, but it was church, and maybe it would do him some good.

Harley looked for our friend Tyler as soon as we got there, and I think he was as pleasantly surprised as I was that she actually came. Of course he could tell right away that she was high. Harley introduced him to Grandma, and we found seats. I was so proud of her for coming, high or not. She was where she needed to be.

Of course Tim had to stir things up. Soon after we got there (the service hadn't started yet), he motioned Harley outside where he was smoking a cigarette and showed her a text on his phone. I went out to see what was going on, and she was absolutely terrified to the point where she said, "Mom, I need to get out of here, now!" She showed me the text that said, "Victoria Hazel Lynn and Tim T. just checked into such and such, a hotel in NYC."

I couldn't understand what the big deal was about, and Harley said, "Mom, that's me. Victoria Hazel Lynn is my Facebook name. It means the guys from NY are going to kill me and Tim, and they posted this message so that when we disappear, everyone will think we're just at some hotel. Tim was actually crying and saying I'm going to be dead by tonight!"

Tyler took Harley aside. The service had started by then, and they were gone quite a while. I don't know what he said to her, but they came back in and she seemed to have calmed down noticeably. I was so glad Tyler had convinced her to stay. Tim had disappeared outside to his car for the remainder of the service, but Harley stayed and actually participated in the Bible readings and prayers. She seemed a lot calmer until she got out to the parking lot, where Tim was waiting.

She and I had planned to spend the day together, but she was so freaked out she insisted I drop her off at a friend's instead, another one whose place she went to a lot that I had a suspicion was dealing drugs and not someone she should be around. The whole drive back, she kept saying she was going to do whatever she had to do to keep us safe, that these people were threatening us (her family) as well as her.

Her battery was dead, so she used my phone to call Grandpa. She was in tears, begging him, "Pop, don't answer the door to any-one! Especially my friends. Including and especially Rick [her friend who was out front after dropping her off and left]." She told him she was with me but she was going to a friend's and she would call him later and explain.

She said, "Promise me you won't let anyone in."

Well, of course he was all upset, wanting to know what was going on, and called me as soon as I got home. I told him the little bit I knew, and he said, "She's high, isn't she?"

I told him yes. I wasn't going to lie to him.

Harley knew he probably wouldn't think twice about answer-ing the door to any of her friends because he had met a lot of them whom she had brought out there before. It was obvious now she didn't know who she could trust.

Betty and Bob had met a lot more of Harley's friends than I had. She never really brought any of them over here with the excep-tion of Tim and her future fiancé Steve, who had convinced her to turn herself in years ago. I was really glad she didn't. With all the drugs she was into, I really didn't want them knowing where I lived.

Different times Betty would tell me how she met this guy or that guy Harley brought over and how nice they seemed. They would tell her how they didn't do drugs, etc. I told her more than once chances were they were only telling her what she wanted to hear, that they were probably providing Harley with the drugs or doing them themselves. Harley later told me how Grandma thought these guys were okay and that they were dealers. I had been around enough of them in my addiction to know.

Chapter

26

I wanted to keep her with me and safe, but against my better judgment, I dropped her off at this friend's house. I couldn't force her to stay with me, knowing from past experience how determined and stubborn she could be. She came by both of those traits through both myself and her dad, unfortunately. I told her to make sure she called me later so I wouldn't worry. Like that would ever happen. I worried about her 24/7.

I was extremely worried that day with this threat. I couldn't help thinking Tim was playing some sort of sick, twisted game. I could tell he seemed jealous of Tyler from the time he found out Tyler was writing to Harley months before. I told her the same thing Betty told her: don't worry about us. God will protect us and he will protect you.

Hours later, she came over to my house with Tim. She didn't come in, just sat in the car in our driveway. She was still all worked up, convinced someone was after them. She handed me her brush and asked me to brush her hair like I did when she was little. She had long beautiful hair, and when I went to brush it for her, a big knot came out.

She yelled, pulled it out of the brush, and handed it to me, saying, "Here, Mom, you'd better keep it for when I'm gone." I told her she wasn't going anywhere and that I didn't ever want to hear her talk that way again. I threw it into the yard beside the car, telling her the birds could use it for a nest.

Right before they left, she said, "Mom, I want you to promise me something: tell John I love him. I hate him, but I love him." That's the very last thing I expected her to say, and it just came out of nowhere. She sounded urgent. "Promise me, Mom, that you'll tell him."

The next few times I saw or talked to her, she seemed fine, as if this whole threat had blown over. It was almost like it never happened.

With working and her doing her own thing, I didn't see her again until December 11. When I gave her the money for the sub-oxone, she had given me a really nice smartphone. I still had the old flip phone I'd had for years, and told her when I got this one hooked up she would have to show me how to use it. She called me that day and asked to borrow it. She said her phone died and she couldn't be without one. Which made no sense because I hadn't activated it yet.

I had gone out that night, and when I got home, I saw Tim's car in the driveway. As I was parking my truck, Harley came running over. She said she brought my phone back and thought I was at work. She had come for the phone that afternoon. She saw my headlights when I pulled in and said to John, "I wonder who that is."

He said, "Probably your mom."

She didn't stay, said Tim was waiting, she had to go. I walked over to his car with her, gave her a hug and kiss, told her I loved her. She slid into the driver's seat, and they left.

Little did I know that would be the last time I saw my baby.

We talked and texted back and forth the following days when I was at work, but that night, on December 11, was the last time I saw her alive. It was always in the back of my mind that we could lose her, but I wouldn't let myself actually believe it because God had always been so faithful in protecting her.

Chapter

27

Tuesday, December 20, 2016, was one of my days off, but the company forced me in to work, not my normal night shift but day shift. It was 12 degrees and bitter cold when I left the house at a little after 5:00 a.m.

I saw I had a text from Betty and assumed she had texted me the night before. I couldn't imagine what she'd be doing up that early. Her text said she was worried about Harley, she couldn't find her. As it turned out, she was up and had sent me the text that morning.

I texted her back, saying, "What do you mean you can't find her?"

I immediately received one back, saying Harley wasn't responding to any of her texts or phone calls. This in turn had me worried. There were a few times in the past where this had happened before, and my baby knew we worried if we didn't hear from her, and especially when she didn't get back to us.

I shot Harley a text myself before I punched in at work, telling her Grandma and I were really worried about her, that she needed to get in touch with me as soon as possible so I knew she was okay. I told her in my text that I was at work and I would check my phone on my breaks. I was thinking later it was lucky I had a cleaning job that day because I could take my own breaks whenever I wanted. I know now it was without a doubt divine intervention.

I work in manufacturing, and we're not supposed to have our cell phones in the actual plant. My phone was always in my locker, so on my first break, I ran up to the locker room and checked for messages. There were none, which had me even more worried.

My second break I took around 10:30 a.m. I had no sooner taken my phone out of my locker than it rang in my hand. It was Harley. I was so relieved! I know God definitely had a hand in all of this that day. What are the chances I'd be able to take my own breaks that day and especially that I took that second break, got to my locker at the exact moment she called?

I told her that Grandma was worried about her too, that she needed to call her. She said she would later, that her phone was about to die. She said, "Mom, I need you to do me a favor. Call John and ask him to pick me up. I'm freezing, and I'm right down the road from your house."

She wanted him to give her a ride somewhere, and to this day, I can't remember where she wanted to go. I hung up and called home right away, asking John to please go get her. He acted like he didn't want to because he knew she was on the run.

I said, "You know how she dresses, or should I say doesn't dress. She never wears a coat. Please, you need to pick her up."

I told him where she said she was, and he said he was leaving right away.

I went outside for a cigarette and took my phone along, which I rarely do. A few minutes later, I got another call from Harley, asking me if John left yet. She said she called the house and there was no answer. I assured her that he had left right after hanging up with me and told her again to be where I told him to go.

I could tell she was high because she was talking over me and I could barely get a word in. I told her I had the next day off but I'd be working overtime, that I had signed up for the following day. I then would be off again Friday and Saturday (Christmas Eve and Christmas).

Before I went back to work, I tried calling Betty to let her know I had just talked to Harley and she was okay. She didn't answer, so I called Bob and asked him to relay the message. I told him John had just left to pick Harley up and told him where. Even knowing John had already left, he too headed out to look for her.

I talked to my husband on my next break. He said he left right away and went down to where Harley said she'd be and she wasn't there. He drove up and down the street where he was to pick her up and all the side streets, drove up to the gas station and got gas being close to empty. He then went back and searched that whole area again, and even went into town to a spot he knew I had picked her up in the past. He never did find her. He said he was out looking for her for almost an hour and a half.

I then called Bob back, and he said he drove all over too, and he was the one to finally find her. He said, "She drives me nuts." He said he took her back home, she got a shower, and he made her something to eat. As soon as she ate, she had Rick, the guy whom she'd been staying with, pick her up.

When I got home from work, I was exhausted, not being used to the day shift. John told me Harley had called him and told him she was sorry she hadn't been where she was supposed to be and thanked him for going out for her anyway. She told him Grandpa found her and she was out there. John said she sounded really good. I wish I had tried to call her when I got home, but Bob had told me her phone died.

Chapter

28

The next morning, I got up fairly early and went to do my grocery shopping. I got home about 12:30 p.m., put everything away, and went up the street to play bingo for a little while. When I left there, I was on my way to pick up my son Brad's Christmas present. I was thinking about trying to call Harley, but I figured I'd wait until I got back and she and I could go do something together, since I had my day off, like I had told her.

I was debating on whether or not to ask her if she wanted her Christmas gift early since she had already given me mine. I was anxious to see her open it, but at the same time, I didn't know if I wanted to give it to her yet as it was only four days until Christmas.

Just as I was thinking I'd try to call her a little later, my phone signaled that I had a text. I thought, "Great, she's texting me. Maybe she'll want to go with me to get her brother's present." I was right up the road from Bob's, wondering if maybe she was out there.

It wasn't Harley. Betty had texted me, "Call me ASAP!"

I called her right away, and I could tell she was crying, but I wasn't at all prepared for what she had to tell me. As soon as she said, "Harley," I thought she was going to say they picked her up and she was back in jail. We were all looking forward to having her home with us for Christmas this year.

Just as I was thinking this she said, "Died. Harley . . . died!"

I think I went completely numb. I just couldn't wrap my mind around what she had just told me. I will *never* get her words and the way she said them out of my head. I remember saying, "What?" and yelling, "No no no!"

She said, "About an hour ago."

But I think that was just the time they pronounced her. It was early afternoon, and Bob had gone shopping too and to pay some bills. He had left pretty early too, so it had to probably be about the time I was at the grocery store.

Betty told me Harley had had Rick drop her off at Bob's in the wee hours of that morning. I told Betty I was going out there, and she said they wouldn't let me in because they were doing an investigation.

I said, "I don't care, I'm heading out there now."

I called my mom, and I was crying so hard she didn't know who it was. I got out there and skidded to a stop alongside the ambulance in the yard. With that and the state police cars, there was nowhere to park. I ran across the yard, screaming, "I want to see my daughter!"

Like Betty had said, they told me I couldn't go in.

I said, "I'm not leaving till I see my daughter!"

They asked Bob to come out, and I gave him a hug. When he went back into the house, I paced the yard, calling the rest of my family, Tyler, and my minister. I was shaking from shock and the freezing temperature. I think my tears froze on my cheeks, and all I could think was how Harley had just said the day before that she was freezing.

I called my minister, as I said, and told him. He had met Harley when she went to church with me one Sunday, and he had gone to see her when she was in jail. I told him how God had always put someone there to save her before. I said, "Where is he now?"

He said of course no one can answer that, but he said if he were to guess he thinks God took her home to get her out of all the pain she was in from the addiction. I told him I knew she was saved when she was little, but I said, "With the lifestyle she was leading, is that any guarantee she's in heaven?"

And he said, "Yes. Once you're saved, you're saved."

I had to leave an urgent message for my daughter Steph, my son Brad, and Tyler. Steph and Tyler called me back, saying they would be there soon, but I didn't see my son until he got there. He works the night shift too and had been sleeping. He's usually up anyway, so I kept calling, and finally, out of frustration and being at the breaking point, I just blurted it out in a message. A lot of times he never gets back to me, so I had to let him know what happened.

He was always begging her to get help too. He worried about her all the time too. He had lost a good friend a year before to a heroin overdose; she was in her early twenties. When I told Harley Brad's friend had died, she said "Mom, she was a friend of mine too."

It wasn't until probably a week later that it dawned on me no one had ever been able to get any cell reception out there anywhere on the property. I had always had to drive up the road before I could get any service. Of all the calls I made from the yard that day, I had crystal clear reception with every single one of them. That never happened! I see God's hand at work everywhere, looking back on all that happened then and in the days ahead.

When I got that phone call, my faith was pretty much shattered. After all the times she had OD-ed before and God had put someone there to save her, I thought sure she was going to eventually get it together and be able to help other addicts with her story of all she had been through. I can't understand why none of us sensed that something was horribly wrong.

My husband called me and came out before Steph or Tyler got there. Betty had a flat tire up the road and got there about the same time John did. Soon after they arrived, the paramedics rolled a gurney up to the door. I was told I could see my baby when they were done investigating.

I was under the impression I could go in when they were finished. Instead, I saw the white body bag as they carried her out. She looked so tiny through that bag. I leaned over and gave her a hug and kiss through the bag and just broke down. I wanted to open the zipper and see her, but something held me back. I swear she still felt warm through that bag. It was all just so surreal—this didn't happen!

I tearfully told her I loved her, and they took her over to the waiting ambulance. Not long after, Tyler pulled in just as the trooper was talking to us. He talked to Tyler too and then gave Betty and I his card, and told us he was going to do everything he could to find out who sold her that fatal bag.

Steph finally showed up and my son Brad. My mom came with all my grandchildren and Jim, Harley's dad, came out. This is a parent's absolute worst nightmare. Jim lost both his children not quite a year and a half apart, and Betty and Bob lost both their granddaughters. Neither Harley nor Macey had any children of their own.

I can't begin to imagine how Bob must feel being the one to find her, again. He had tried CPR, like he did that first time, but it was too late. If he had been able to get her heart pumping again, we may have had the unimaginable horror of having to take her off life support, which would have been so much worse. I hope Bob realizes it wasn't his fault.

Rick, the friend whom she had been staying with who picked her up the day before, took her out to Grandpa's in the wee hours of that morning. Bob said she was high as a kite. I'm guessing on meth since that's what he was into, but it could have been heroin, I don't know. Harley was always a night owl, and he said by about 6:00 a.m. that day she was absolutely fine.

They were going to get some sleep, and Bob told her when he got up he was going to go to the store, he'd see her when he got back. She had said, "Okay, love you, Pop," and went into her room. He said he had left her a note and when he got back it had been moved, so he knew she had been up at some point.

Everything was quiet when he returned, so he figured she had gone back to bed. He put his groceries away before going in to see if she wanted bacon with her eggs, and he couldn't wake her up. He did CPR, like he had done that first time he found her, but it was too late. She was gone. I can't help thinking in a way that may have been a blessing, considering if he had been able to get her heart pumping again, we may have had to make the horrific decision of having to take her off life support.

Chapter

29

I had arrived out at Bob's around 2:00 p.m. that day and didn't get back home until after 8:00 p.m., after everyone else had left Bob's. I was still very much in a state of shock and disbelief. I couldn't sit still. I was up and down, pacing back and forth.

I finally said to John, "For the first time in over sixteen years, I want to get a damn bottle. I need something for my nerves."

I paced back to the bedroom before coming back out and telling him I was going. It wasn't until the next day he told me he had taken my keys. He said, "After all you went through with her when she was alive and you didn't drink, you're not going to start now."

I think the only thing that really stopped me was the fact that Harley had often told me how proud she was of me for cleaning my life up and knowing she wouldn't have wanted that. I probably would have lost everything—my job, my house. I was never one to be able to drink just one and be done with it. I would have been back right where I left off, in full-blown alcoholic mode with no end in sight.

I already felt as though I had lost everything. I've never been suicidal, but I said, "Lord, I don't want to live in a world my baby's no longer a part of."

All the drugs her dad and I did over the years, it should have been one of us. I would have gladly traded my life for hers. She had her whole life ahead of her, she and Macey.

John gave me one of his muscle relaxers, and it wasn't until 2:00 or 3:00 a.m. that I was able to finally lie down and get a few hours of sleep, only to be smacked with the awful truth of what had happened the minute I awoke.

The next two days were pretty much a blur. Three days after we lost her, we had to have the service because of having her cremated. On Christmas Eve, of all days! My oldest granddaughter, Taylor, seemed to take it harder than the other girls and called me in tears, saying, "Grammy, it's Christmas Eve, why do we have to do it today?"

We had a private viewing and a small service. It was family only, with the exception of Tyler and Sandy from my Bible study. I didn't want any of her dealer "friends" showing up. Tim wanted to be there, and I told him flat out, "No! You were a big part of the problem!"

I only found out later that he was the last person to talk to her at 6:00 a.m. that day. When I asked him why he called her and what was said, he told me, "I just called to ask her if she was still alive."

Seriously? Who does that? The state troopers had questioned him, but they said aside from him being a little weird, they didn't think he had anything to do with her death. Yet he was obsessed with both Macey and Harley, and they're both gone.

I had asked my minister if he would come, and he said he'd be honored. I feel so bad that I didn't invite Marilyn, my friend the prison chaplain. I was in no way thinking clearly and somehow neglected to do that. She had called me, and we talked for a while, but I think that was afterward.

I believe I mentioned that my oldest, Steph, hooked up with one of Harley's friends they got their heroin from, and Steph insisted he was coming to the service with her, that he was her support and he needed to see her so he could get some closure. I told her no, he wasn't. He wasn't welcome there, and she would just have to respect my wishes. I told the funeral director I was afraid she'd cause a scene, and he said if I gave him a list of the people coming and Josh wasn't on it, he would see that he wasn't allowed in.

It was beyond hard. My minister performed a beautiful service, and Betty and I got up and said a few words. My youngest granddaughter, Jewlia, got up and shared a memory of how Harley had protected them when they were scared. Taylor threw herself across Harley and hugged her. The whole thing was just heartbreaking.

Jim's girlfriend, Heidi, wrapped her arms around me and held me at the end. I kept saying, "I don't want to let her go." She said, "I know." She and Jim have been together since Harley was little, and although they're not married, Harley always referred to her as her stepmom.

My husband had tears in his eyes, and my son said to him, "It's okay to cry, John." When he was so hard on her, he would always say, "It's called tough love." I think he really feels bad about the way he treated her sometimes. Just recently, he told me he thinks about her all the time. I told him she would have loved to have heard him say that.

When we had to leave, I gave my baby a kiss and told her how much I loved her. It's without a doubt the hardest thing I've ever had to do in my life. Looking back, I wish I had asked the funeral director for a lock of her long, beautiful hair, but of course, at the time, that was the furthest thing from my mind.

Chapter

30

One of the last texts I sent Harley, I asked her if she wanted to go with me to the candlelight Christmas Eve service at Tyler's church, where she had just gone with us on December 4. She never really did answer me, and I wanted to ask her again when I saw her but never got that chance. I think she would have if this hadn't happened. She had a lot of questions about God when we were out at the pool one day. Right before Grandpa bailed her out and right before she met Tyler, she said, "Mom, please tell Tyler to write me. I need to get right with God."

I had really looked forward to her hopefully going with me that night. Instead, we were saying good-bye to her just hours before. I go to the Christmas Eve service every year, and even under the circumstances, I strongly felt that I needed to be there. I knew I needed that constant connection with God.

Betty came over to my house soon after the service and stayed the rest of the day intending to go with me, but at the last minute she said she needed to go home and make her pies for the next day. I knew my husband wouldn't go; he never did. I really didn't want to go by myself, but I felt I needed to be there in God's house.

When we lit the candles and sang, "Silent night, rest in heavenly peace," the tears were just streaming down my face. Afterward,

Tyler told me his minister wanted to pray with me. He remembered seeing Harley with us that Sunday.

No one felt like celebrating Christmas. We always go to my mom's house for dinner and to exchange gifts, and she said, too, she didn't feel like having anything, but we both agreed we needed to be with family. I felt this little voice nudging me to make a quick detour to Betty and Bob's on the way. I told them I thought Harley would have wanted me to stop and give them all a hug. Her dad and uncle Tom have always gone out there for Christmas dinner, just as my family always went to my parents' house.

All together with my three bereavement days from work, two personal days I hadn't used before, and the holidays, I was off work for about eleven days, and I really dreaded going back. I knew it was going to be hard with people coming up to me.

When I opened my locker, there was a card inside. Not from my crew—they didn't bother, which really hurt—but from a good friend of mine in my department, only on a different shift. A lot of people on her crew signed it, people I had worked with before we went to the twelve hours. I have a Brinks lock on there and couldn't imagine how she got it in there, but it really touched me.

I found out later by someone who watched her do it that she struggled to wedge it in the little louvers at the top. That was a complete surprise, and very much appreciated. Surprisingly, only one or two people came up to me and offered any kind of condolences that night. I didn't know whether to be relieved or upset that it seemed no one cared.

Somehow, I got through that first night back. I have a video of my baby on my phone that Tim made up of pictures of her after she passed away, along with the song someone did in memory of Paul Walker. I don't even know the name of it. It's beautiful but so sad. Tim made it, as I said, and much as I blame him for everything, it really is a beautiful video that he put on the Internet. I think he may have loved Harley in his own strange way. But I think *obsessed* would be a better word.

None of us had any life insurance on Harley, and even after being told he couldn't come to the service, he asked if he could help with the cost. He gave me $500, which really did help at the time. I didn't want anything to do with him, but I feel he had everything to do with what happened. He never tried to talk her into getting the help she desperately needed. He owed it to her to help now. Maybe I'm wrong to think like that, but there you have it, those were my feelings at the time, whether they made any sense or not.

I took my phone out to my car on several of my breaks and watched this video. There are some beautiful pictures of my daughter I had never seen before. I sat there in my car watching this and bawling my eyes out. It was still so hard to comprehend that she really was gone. It still doesn't seem real a little over a year later. I can be fine one minute and having a meltdown the next. The grief just hits me out of the blue all over again with the force of a freight train. I've experienced quite a few of these meltdowns on my way home from work and almost had to pull over a few times. I was crying so hard I was having trouble seeing the road. I feel like my heart's been ripped out.

I couldn't ask for a nicer or more understanding boss. My second night back, he took me aside and had a long talk with me. He said he didn't say anything the night before because he figured I'd be bombarded by everyone and overwhelmed.

He said he got a call from his mother at work five years ago. She always called him on his birthday and sang "Happy Birthday" to him. He was busy at the time and didn't call her back right away. When he did, she told him his brother had been found dead of a heroin overdose behind the restaurant where he worked. That must have been horrible for him, for all of them.

He said she just gave up after that. He told me if there was anything I needed—time off anytime or whatever—to just let him know. He said, "I know what my mom went through." He even tried to get Harley's video on the Internet onto a DVD for me.

Chapter

31

I know my minister told me, "Once you're saved, you're saved," but I kept worrying about this, human nature being what it is. I guess you could say I needed more concrete reassurance (the enemy attacking). I kept praying, "Lord, please show me some sort of a sign that she's up there with you."

One night, as I was on my way to work, I had just reached the exact spot where I had been when my whole world shattered, and I just happened to look up at the sky. There over the lake was a perfect sideways cross! If that's not my sign, I don't know what is.

Before that one night, John was watching TV as I was getting ready for work, and there was some sort of commercial on. All I heard was these words, and I've never seen or heard it since, which is really weird. It said, "I'm home, I'm home, I'm home!"

I remember thinking, "I wonder if that's my sign," but more or less dismissed it right away. I couldn't imagine God using the TV as my sign. But who knows, he is the God of miracles and can use anything to get our attention.

In the days, weeks, and months to come, God put so many people in my path to offer me comfort or a shoulder to cry on, including two women whom I work with who had lost their young sons. The one Harley knew and the other one his mother told me Harley died on his birthday. In addition to that, I received cards and phone calls from people whom I hadn't heard from in years. There was just such an outpouring of warmth and compassion, some from people I work with but didn't even know.

The company union presented me with a beautiful comfort edition Bible with the inscription "In Loving Memory of Harley Lynn Harlan." I received a nice basket of assorted plants from the company itself. My one friend whose son died has a picture of Jesus holding and looking at her son's picture on her locker next to mine, and I had asked her where she got it. I had gone into work one night after a particularly rough night the night before, thinking about my baby and having one of my meltdowns. I saw out of the corner of my eye while opening my locker a picture of Jesus on it and thinking it had fallen off Michelle's locker and was accidentally put on mine.

I reached for it and realized it wasn't the picture of her son but of Harley. I cried when I saw it and knew she had done this for me.

Soon after that, I was in the breakroom one night when another Christian friend of mine came up to me and handed me an envelope and just walked away, went back to work. It was another beautiful gesture. She and her husband had purchased two children's books from a local library and donated them in my daughter's name. She told me later rather than flowers that wouldn't last they decided to do this for me so her name will live on through other children who read them. I told her it was an awesome gesture and how much Harley would have liked that, considering how much she loved kids and loved to read.

Chapter

32

Less than a month after losing my daughter, I woke up one morning on my first day off, which was a Monday. I was immediately hit with the realization that Mondays were the nights my old church group went into the prison to do their service with the women. This was definitely God's hand at work again; there is just no other explanation for it.

That was my first thought upon awakening whereas I hadn't thought about it in years. I hadn't been involved in the prison ministry in probably six years because of my work schedule. I hadn't given it a thought when we started working the twelve hours and having days off. Those were special times I looked forward to spending time with Harley. It wasn't until days later that I realized they only go in once a month and this just happened to be their Monday.

That evening, I called one of the women in the group, and she was literally on her way out the door to go to the prison. That wasn't my timing, it was the Lord's. When I asked her if I could join them, she said, "Absolutely. I will meet you out front in a few minutes." She said that if I thought it was too soon and changed my mind after hanging up to text her she would understand.

The minute I hung up the phone, I burst into tears, thinking "It is too soon, I can't do this!" At the same time, I felt God s strong but gentle nudge, saying, "Yes, Candy, you can. If you don't do this now, when and if you ever get around to it, a lot of the women who knew Harley will have been released."

When we went into the chapel, Marilyn, the prison chaplain, took one look at me, and I swear her jaw dropped. She put her arms around me and said she had been thinking about asking me to come in, but like Lori said, she thought it would be too soon. Then she got this serious look on her face and said, "Oh no, it's been so long since the last time you were in that you no longer have clearance. Hopefully no one will bother us. Do you see how God brought all of this together?"

The women filed in soon after. I saw a few who had been serving time with me all those years ago, and my heart went out to them that they still hadn't gotten it right. But they were in church, definitely a step in the right direction. Marilyn offered to sit up front with me and explained to the women that they had a very special guest, Harley's mom. Most of them had known my daughter, as I had suspected, and had of course heard that she had recently passed away.

I told them all how they all had so much to live for, that they could change their lives around while they still had the chance and begged those of them that were into the drugs, particularly the heroin or knew anyone who was, to do everything in their power to get themselves or that other person help while they still had a life.

When it was time for them to go back, they all gave me a hug, thanked me for coming, and told me stories about about my baby, how she used to entertain them. One woman told me Harley actually saved her life. I didn't have time to get any details, but I told her I was glad Harley had been there for her.

Another woman came up to me and asked me if I remembered her from way back, one of my first stays in there. I told her, "Yes, of course I remember you." Her name was also Candy. I had met her brother a few years before when we were both working as temps, and he had told me she was into the heroin but had been doing good the last time I talked to him.

I went home that night completely drained, but as I got into my car, I felt so much better than I ever expected I would. I had cried my heart out while trying my best to get through to them, and it was like I experienced God's awesome sense of peace flow over me. I felt as though a heavy load had been lifted.

Marilyn has her office door and a wall in the chapel covered with pictures of women and newspaper articles of women, myself included, who have been in there at one time or another. When I went in that night, I saw the women had a broken heart, with Macey's name on it, and next to it they had added Harley's. I later gave Marilyn pictures of the two of them together to add to the rest.

Chapter

33

The state police were still conducting their investigation into Harley's death, and Betty and I kept after them, telling them she needed justice and in no way did we want this to become a cold case. We took any information we had to them, and they had her cell phone they were going through.

One day, we got tired of not hearing anything, so we paid a visit to the barracks. The trooper in charge told us it was a slow process, and he couldn't share any details with us. He did say that at that point they had it narrowed down to two people who sold her that deadly bag and he was very hopeful they would get that person responsible.

Weeks went by and, I called him again. We were getting beyond frustrated. I left a message for the trooper in charge, telling him I needed a progress update. He returned my call that night, asking me to meet him at the barracks, that he needed to talk to me. He said he had also called Betty and Bob, so we drove out together.

I had heard days before that Harley's "friend" who had dropped her off the night before she died had been arrested and was in the county prison. I was so sure they were going to tell us it had been him and that they were charging him with her death.

We were so hopeful going in there that this was it, they had gotten my baby justice at last. Instead, we were totally blindsided with yet another devastating blow. As soon as we sat down, we were told how sorry they were but they couldn't charge *anyone* with her death. The coroner's report had finally come back, and the toxicology results showed that there were five or six different drugs in her system, so they were unable to determine which one actually caused her death. She hadn't done them all at once; some drugs stay in the system longer than others.

Yet with all this new advanced technology, I can't understand why they weren't able to isolate which one she had done last. There is absolutely no doubt in my mind that it was the heroin laced with fentanyl, two of which were on that list.

There had been a big drug bust involving heroin the year before, where it was being packaged in a garage in town—a huge operation, about the first and second time Harley OD-ed. So I'm thinking maybe she did actually did get justice for those times. We live in a small city where if you're into the drugs, everybody knows everybody.

With an operation of that scale, chances are better than not that that's where she got it. Those people got quite a bit of time. If it weren't for the Narcan and the grace of God, she would have died either of those times. If Bob hadn't gotten that gut feeling and stayed home that first time, Harley would have died before Macey.

I still had three voice mails on my old phone from Harley that I have since transferred onto a cassette tape so I wouldn't lose them. Something told me when I received them in November (a month before) and one in December (a matter of weeks before we lost her) not to delete them. My finger was on the delete button—I always deleted my messages after listening to them—when something told me not to. I'm so glad I didn't delete them. Hard as they are to listen to, I'm glad I have them.

There are so many what-ifs. For example, looking back, I sometimes think that was God's voice telling me not to. There was a reason I wasn't supposed to delete those messages. Why didn't I realize I had that feeling because she wouldn't be with us much longer?

These kinds of thoughts pop into my head and torment me at times. I need to let go and let God. All these regrets are doing nothing but destroy me if I let them. There is nothing we can do to change the past. All we can do is try our best to forgive ourselves and somehow live our lives until we see her again. I know she wouldn't want us to keep beating ourselves up.

Her dad is having a really hard time as well. I'm sure he's probably beating himself up as well for much of the same reasons, all the lost time he could have had with our daughter, as well as Macey. Betty told me he has their pictures all over his dresser, that his girls are the last thing he sees before going to bed and the first thing he sees when he wakes up.

God forgives us. To not find a way to forgive ourselves is like saying Jesus died in vain. She was (all children) are a precious gift from God; they are only on loan to us. I never really thought about that before. Everything we have comes from him. For reasons I will never understand until I can ask him someday, he thought it best to call her home way too soon.

The day I picked up her ashes and brought her home, I said, "Oh, baby, I always wanted you to live with me again, but not like this, never like this."

Five months later, in the spring, when the ground had finally begun to thaw, my son Brad and I went up to my dad's grave and buried some of Harley's ashes with him, my grandparents, and my aunt. I fell apart the first time I took flowers up there after that. It never gets any easier. I miss them so much.

My granddaughters, Harley's nieces, wanted locket necklaces with her ashes in, so I ordered four of them through a catalog, one for myself as well. The tiny urn inside is about the size and shape of a bullet, which made them very tedious to fill. John cut a razor-sharp edge on a drinking straw so I could scoop them up and pour them in easily.

There's a beautiful worship song that came to mind as I steeled myself to do this: "I Can Only Imagine." I listened to it as I filled the urns. It especially came to mind remembering how Harley, when she was little, proclaimed that one day she was going to dance for Jesus!

I could just, and still can, picture her doing just that. If you've never heard this song, it goes like this:

I Can Only Imagine

I can only imagine what it will be like. When I walk by your side. I can only imagine what my eyes will see, when your face is before me. I can only imagine.

Surrounded by your Glory, what will my heart feel? Will I dance for you Jesus? Or in awe of you be still? Will I stand in your presence or to my knees will I fall? Will I sing Hallelujah? Will I be able to speak at all? I can only imagine, I can only imagine.

I can only imagine when that day comes. And I find myself standing in the sun. I can only imagine when all I will do Is forever, forever worship you. I can only imagine, yeah. I can only imagine . . .

I could just picture my beautiful daughter standing in God's presence, seeing her jaw drop as she stood in awe of him, before doing just as she said she would and dancing for Jesus. It brings me great comfort knowing she's wrapped in our Savior's loving arms, surrounded by all our family members who had gone on before. I'm sure she was welcomed with loving arms by each and every one.

Both hers and Macey's lives were cut way too short. Although I could see the very real pain she was in with this horrible addiction, knowing she's now pain-free and no doubt happier than she's ever been brings me some semblance of comfort.

A lot of the beautiful heartfelt poems that she wrote spoke of all that pain and a lot about God himself. After her death, Betty found her (Betty's) Daily Bread devotional under her sofa, where Harley would sleep when she was there. She said apparently she would read it a lot when she stayed overnight because each page Harley had dog-eared.

I have one of her many letters she had written to me while incarcerated only a short time before she came home for the last time. She said she wanted so bad to go back to the life she once had, to get clean. She wanted to go back to school (college) and get to know her nieces again. To make something of her life. I always told her she could do whatever she set her mind to.

There is so much on her Facebook (she went by Victoria Hazel Lynn) that I had never seen before. I later found a lot of things on her page once I got a phone with Internet. She spoke of how she wanted to make us all proud by getting her life back on track and not having to look over her shoulder anymore. That she vowed to do that before it was too late. She had planned to check herself into a rehab once the holidays were over. She was looking forward to being home with us for Christmas, as she had spent the previous Christmas behind bars once again.

I have so many precious memories that I will always hold dear. Everything reminds me of her: movies she liked, books, places we went together, songs—the list goes on and on. Years ago, Steph made me a CD of my favorite songs Harley and I always listened to when we were in the car. One song, called "Last Kiss," she liked as much as I did. She was singing it out on my pool deck the summer before she passed away. It goes like this: "Where oh where can my baby be? The Lord took her away from me. She's gone to Heaven so I've got to be good, so I can see my baby when I leave this world."

It's taken on a whole new meaning since she died. I can very rarely bring myself to listen to it anymore. There's a song too from a Leonardo DiCaprio movie called *Catch Me if You Can*. I've only heard it once since Harley's been gone. It came on when I was driving one day, and I looked up to the heavens and said, "Baby, here's your song." Being on the run all the time, it just seemed like it was written for her.

When Harley was little, she would call Betty "Gamma" and Bob "Poppy." In later years, she shortened them to "Gram" and "Pop." My mother she always called "G." She was the only one of my children who called me "Mama." It sounded so cute. I loved that.

Her dad worked in pizza shops, and I was in the manufacturing business, shoe factories all my life until the last one I worked at shut down. Harley would run around the house and in a singsong voice say, "Mommy makes shoes and boots, Daddy makes pizza!"

Chapter

34

There is no greater pain than that of losing a child. It leaves a horrible void that nothing can fill. A huge part of me died with her that day. I would give anything in this world to have her back or just to have one more day with her. She is basking in Jesus's love, receiving more love from her Heavenly Father than any of us could ever give her on this earth. Every time the pain of missing her becomes unbearable, I picture her wrapped in his arms.

I started going to a grief-share support group at my church on my days off. My boss said to let him know what days I needed for it and I could just come in to work late on those nights. It was awesome that he was willing to do that for me, but after the very first one, I told him I didn't know if it was for me.

The initial one I did go to, even after being able to open up and talk to the women in the prison, I just couldn't. The entire two hours I just sat there with the tears streaming down my face. I made up my mind to try it again on my next day off, and it went a little better from there on. I think it did help somewhat.

I met a woman in there one night who had lost her nineteen-year-old daughter Tori while in the county prison. She had been going through withdrawal from heroin and by no means got the proper treatment. She has a huge lawsuit pending against the prison.

Harley had told me she saw how she was being treated; she was in there herself when it happened.

I didn't know until later that Stephanie, Tori's mother, had been writing to Harley. She contacted me on Facebook after Harley died, telling me she had a poem Harley wrote and sent to her that she thought I'd like to have.

One night months later, I met her in my grief group, and she brought me the poem and some letters Harley had written to her. Our group takes a few months' break and then starts up again, so we've been keeping in touch in between. I'm glad she was there for Harley.

One of the things I've learned in grief share is that we need to lean on and get our strength from God one day at a time. The Word for Today, one of my favorite devotionals, really spoke to what I'm going through the other day.

This particular reading for the day said, "Let the mistakes go." Allow yourself to be free, and learn to forgive yourself by receiving with an open heart God's total and complete forgiveness. Stop beating yourself up, because Jesus took all your beatings at the cross. Stop punishing yourself, because Jesus took all the punishment for you. I pray every day for the healing of our broken hearts and thank God every day for the time I did have with my beautiful daughter.

Our children are precious gifts from God. Everything we have is God's, including our children, who are really only on loan to us. Eventually we have to give them back to the Lord, who created them. We will all die sometime, but we never expect our children to go before us.

Harley wrote us all a lot of letters while behind bars, and she had a really unique signature: "Always, Harley." She would draw a heart around and through the *always*. I had a tattoo done on my forearm of her exact signature. I'm really happy with it, and I think she would have loved it; she had quite a few tattoos of her own.

Chapter

35

Soon after we lost her, I contacted an attorney, fully intending to file a lawsuit against the county probation office. They were supposed to have a detainer on her to prevent her from getting out on bail. She knew this, and it's why she never went to her last court hearing and instead was on the run again from the day she got out. She knew if she had shown up in court they would have realized they dropped the ball and she would have been right back in. If they had done their job, she would still be alive.

My attorney was willing to take the case, but I never got back to him. The more I thought about it, the more I realized I couldn't in all good conscience pursue it because it wasn't just them—we were all at fault. I had turned her in twice in the past when I saw how out of control she was getting, and I was afraid for her. I couldn't just sit back and do nothing.

I never reported her myself. I had a friend of mine do it because I was afraid she'd hate me if she knew I had done it. I really believe if I hadn't she would have died a lot sooner. I just can't believe I didn't see how bad she was getting this last time. I should have seen the signs. If one of us had turned her in, she would still be alive. John said different times he wanted to, but he didn't because of me. Now I really wish he had.

Chapter

36

I keep thinking of things we could have done together and things I wish I had told her. Every time we'd see each other or talk on the phone though, we'd always say, "I love you," and that was so important, something you can never say enough because you just never know if it could be for the last time.

She had her whole life ahead of her. There were so many things she never got to experience in her short life. She had her permit and drove all the time, but she never got her license—that was one of the things I found on her list of goals. She never had her own apartment or her own car. All she wanted was to get away from the drugs and be happy.

She was so looking forward to Nate (the love of her life) getting out so they could get married and start a family. She wanted kids so bad! She just wanted to go back to having a normal life, and she had so much love to give. She wanted to go back to school and make something of herself. She always loved animals (particularly tigers) and often said she thought maybe she'd like to become a veterinarian.

My heart just breaks for what could have been and all the time I lost with her that I can never get back. I just have to seek comfort in the fact that she's free now. Like Betty says, as much as we want her here with us, she wouldn't want to come back.

I'm just so thankful for the time I did have with her and that she didn't suffer. That she was out at Grandpa's. If she hadn't been, who knows where or if she would have been found?

I just don't want her death to be in vain. I'm hoping and praying her story will help save someone else and their family from going through the hell we've been through. This unfathomable and profound loss, I wouldn't wish this kind of pain on my worst enemy.

Chapter

37

There are millions of addicts out there. This horrible disease touches people in all walks of life. So many people look down on addicts and say it's their own fault, it's all about choices. Yes, it is all about choices, but this horrific epidemic can affect anyone. No one grows up saying they want to be an addict.

The heroin is especially hard to get away from once you're in its grips. Addicts love the high, but it instills a sense of hopelessness and shame. Like all addicts, I'm sure Harley had a love-hate relationship with the drug. She broke all her syringes in half in front of Betty one day, saying, "Gramma, I'm done, I hate this stuff."

Speaking from my own experience as a recovering addict, when a person is in the grips of an addiction, that addict is literally out there. Every waking moment is consumed with chasing that high; it's basically the only thing that matters. With the heroin, it's so much worse because they have to have it all the time in order to avoid becoming deathly sick.

A decent loving person can be driven to do whatever they have to get it, things they would never ordinarily do. I sure did a lot of things I'm not proud of that went against everything I was ever taught. Harley once said to me, "Mom, if you knew some of the things I've done, you wouldn't love me." I assured her that that wasn't true. I told her, "Nothing could ever stop me from loving you."

Addiction does *not* define a person, it's not who they are. I once told her I wanted my loving, considerate child back, and she said, "Mom, she died a long time ago with the rape and all I've been through." I told her that wasn't true, that she was still in there somewhere.

I just read an article in the newspaper the other day about another beautiful young girl who had died of a heroin overdose and her mother is raising her two children. Her mother said, "The person you loved is still in there somewhere, clouded and obscured by the haze of addiction." I couldn't have said it better myself.

I just recently connected with a local artist who lost his brother to heroin three years ago, and he is bringing awareness to our city by doing projections on buildings. A picture on the front page of the paper caught my eye one day as it was a picture of the funeral home where we did Harley's service. He did a projection on the front of the building that stated, "Overdose + Death = Homicide."

I contacted him on his Facebook address, told him about Harley, and asked him if he would be willing to do a projection of her picture along with a message to the community. He got back to me saying he would be honored. He is in the process of putting it together now and will let me know when he plans on showing it.

My son Brad and I went to one he did where he had Fox 43 News come out, and Brad and I did an interview with them. I sent a message to the dealers out there, saying, "I pray every day you don't get a moment's peace knowing my daughter's gone because of you. Would you give this poison you're selling to our kids to your own kids?"

For those of you interested in this fight and making a difference, check out what Adam DelMarcelle is doing on Facebook at What Heroin Sounds Like.

I never before even considered writing a book, but I've felt God laying this on my heart almost from the beginning. This is my way of being able to do something for Harley and at the same time reach out to others who are hurting or going through what she went thru, what we all are going through. I feel she can help others by my telling her story.

I was overwhelmed with the idea at first because I didn't have a clue as to go about having it published, but I felt I should just do it and I would cross that bridge once I was done. As always, God is faithful. Not long ago, everything just fell into place.

I told my minister, my grief-share group, and a few of my friends and family that I wanted to do this as a way of keeping my baby's memory alive and reaching out to and hopefully helping others. Everyone I talked to about it thought it was a great idea, and they've been very encouraging.

When I told Tyler (Harley's and my friend from work), he too thought it was a great idea and often asks me, "How's the book coming?" He asked me on break one night if I was going to include the part about Ephesians 6. I wasn't sure exactly what he was referring to, so I asked him to write down whatever he would like me to include.

He has a tablet he uses to write to the men in prison on his breaks, and he must have gotten it out and gone right to work on it. I was working an hour or two later, and he had a sheet he printed out and brought over to my department. I sat there and cried as I read it. This is what he gave me:

> It's by God's merciful yet jealous character that even in the midst of Harley's chaotic life, he valiantly pursued her undivided attention. The Lord knew there was a childlike faith still alive in her and yearning to be released from the bondage of the world. Mine and Harley's relationship was progressing at a rapid pace, and the soil of her heart was beginning to be cultivated so more and more seeds could germinate, but the more progress she made, the more the enemy began pressing in.
>
> I remember the time Harley finally came to church with me. We spent the first half of the service outside she was shaking and crying, fearful for her life, and I was praying over her. Her tears dried up, and we went back inside at the right

time to hear the pastor begin to speak about the armor of God, referencing Ephesians 6.

With excitement, she passed me a note saying that someone told her to read Ephesians 6. She'd come to the point now where she had no doubt God was alive and working, despite the trials she was going through, and also convinced there were no such things as coincidences.

Myself, on the other hand, could almost plainly see what was about to happen; there would be another trial, but God was trying to tell her to arm herself for battle. I was excited that something was materializing, and this was confirmation she was hearing from the Lord and that I could pour into her more.

We met the next day for breakfast. Finally, we were having genuine and honest, groundbreaking conversation as our omelets sat there getting cold. The spiritual side of things from the heavenly realms began making sense to her as Ephesians 6 talks about.

I reminded her of the Word I received for her while writing back and forth while she was in county jail: "You're a leader of women," in simplest terms. I was counting on that Word flourishing. After our conversation, I took her back to the place she was staying. A little over a week later, I got the horrific voice mail saying she had died.

We do not battle flesh and blood. I had the privilege of seeing from God's perspective, always looking at her with unconditional love, and I love what God wanted for her. If it weren't for Christ's love, we would've never met, and I wouldn't have been able to see her as God sees her.

Though she had a powerful anointing on her life that made her a big target for the snares of the enemy, the principle of sowing and reaping still applies. Oftentimes, the more powerful the anointing, the harder the opposition. I took comfort in Ephesians 6 after she passed. There have been several attacks on me and some of her family since then, mainly questions of "Is she saved?"

In reflecting on her death, we ought to take captive any thought that doesn't align with what God knows to be true, that faith of a mustard sees as a little child sealed her once and for all, Christ died for her once and for all, and she is living with him in paradise for all eternity. Yes, we all fall short of God's glory, but while we were still a long way off, our Heavenly Father welcomes us with open arms.

In this, I have peace. Until we meet again, I will miss my sister in Christ.

Chapter

38

I can't stress enough how horrific this disease is. This epidemic has gotten way out of control, and I, for one, would like to find ways to help in any way I can. We are losing so many of our young people. Our next generation is being wiped out due to all these senseless heroin/opioid deaths.

To all of you struggling addicts out there, as well as your families, my heart and ceaseless prayers go out to each and every one of you. Please do whatever you have to do to get the help you need, and follow through with whatever you are told to do to get and stay clean. I won't tell you it's easy, it's anything but. What I can tell you is that it is well worth it to get your life back. Contrary to what a lot of people think, you cannot do it alone.

Parents, if like me you are out there using, please take a good hard look at what you're doing to yourselves and your children. This disease doesn't just affect you; it affects everyone around you as well, particularly your loved ones. Get the help you so desperately need or help for the people around you who need it.

The thing that really tore at my heart was the fact that Harley, being an adult, there was nothing I could do as far as forcing her into rehab. She had to be the one to do that. It was different with me when Betty and Bob court ordered me into one because of my daughter being in my care at the height of my addiction.

As parents, the best thing you can do for your children is to talk to them about the dangers of addiction at the earliest age where they will understand. Bring them up on God's Word, and above all, be there for them when they need you, and even when they don't. Love them with everything you have, and spend quality time with them. Life can be gone in an instant, and it will *never* be the same.

Harley told me after Macey died that she (Macey) had come to her in a dream and said, "Learn from me."

I'm begging you to learn from Harley. Do whatever, *whatever* you have to while you or your loved ones still have a life!

Left – Harley
Her Sister – Right

Brother Brad – Harley & I
Her last Christmas with us

Harley – 2-3 years old – one of my favorites

Harley & I

Harley

"2010" Harley's Graduation Day in State Prison (GED)

Steve, man I was with before my husband – My mother (G)
Steph (husband) – Mike & Harley
Steph's Wedding Day – I was in Jail

Harley holding her nieces
Left "Taylor" – Middle "Jewlia" – Right "Alissa"

Harley & I
She was 7 or 8

Our Christmas in Heaven

We see the countless Christmas Trees around the world below
with tiny lights, like heaven's stars, reflecting on the snow.
The sight is so spectacular, please wipe away that tear,
For we are spending Christmas with Jesus Christ each year.

We hear the many Christmas songs that people hold so dear,
but the sounds of music can't compare with the Christmas choir up here!
We have no words to tell you, the joy their voices bring,
for it is beyond description to hear the angels sing.

We know how much you miss us, we see the pain inside your heart,
but we are so far away. We really aren't apart.
So be happy for us dear ones. You know we hold you dear
and be glad we are spending Christmas with Jesus Christ each year.

We send you each a special gift from our heavenly home above.
We send you each a memory of our undying love.
After all "Love" is the gift, more precious than pure gold.
It was always most important in the stories Jesus told.

Please love and keep each other, as our Father said to do,
for we can't count the blessings or love He has for you.

So, have a Merry Christmas and wipe away the tears.
Remember, we are spending Christmas with Jesus Christ each year.

Love Always, *Harley and Macey*

School picture 16 yrs. old

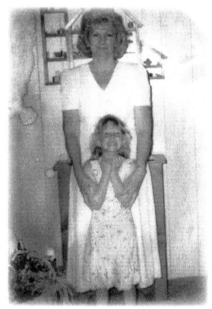

Grandma Betty & Harley
Approx. 6 yrs. old

Left – Harley
Right – Macey

Grandpa Bob – Harley – Macey

Bob, me, Harley, her dad Jim & Betty

Grandpa Bob & Harley
Cambridge Springs
State Prison
2012 Age 22

Macey – Left
Harley – Right

Harley, Macey, Grandma Betty

Harley

Harley – Left
Macey – Right
State Prison visit "2010" Age 20 - Harley
Macey 19

Graduation Age 20 – "2010"
Cambridge Springs State prison
Harley & Grandpa

Harley & Bob's Dog Tinkerbell

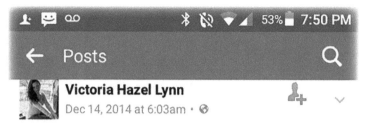

Victoria Hazel Lynn
Dec 14, 2014 at 6:03am · ⊕

Tonight was actually just what I believe I've needed!
Not only have I been able to spend endless hours with
one of the best guys I know, but it's also given me
plenty of thinking time as well.. I just want my life
back, the one I had before I turned 18. The one where
real, genuine happiness was evident simply in just the
way I smiled. Where I wasn't constantly looking over
my shoulder. The life I had with my best friend, who is
now my gorgeous Fiance... I absolutely NEED to get
my shit together before it's too late. For those of yall
that still have faith in me, Even it's just a little, ...
thankyou. Means a helluva lot more to me than any of
yall may even realize! I am going to get better & find
that true happiness that I once had, oh so long ago.
Regardless of what I have to do, I vow to myself & to
my man to not give up hope... I'll eventually get it
right! I have to if it's the last thing I do.. wish me luck!!
☺
Baby we're gunnar make it, believe that no matter
what transpires! We love each other, & in the end
that's all that matters. We can both do anything we
put our minds to. Our relationship is going to grow
beautifully, all I need out of this messed up yet

...rful life is YOU. remember that. I love you baby,
... of me! Forever & always!

& as for Tim.... thank you for being my support

I found this on Harley's Facebook soon after she passed
away and reading what she wrote just broke my heart.

About the Author

C. J. Levan is a first-time author of *Harley's Story: The Life of an Addict*. Her goal is to reach out to other addicts and their families with her daughter's story.

This book was written in loving memory of Harley Lynn Harlan and her battle with addiction. She died of a heroin overdose in 2016.

C. J. Levan is striving to bring awareness to this horrific epidemic, and it is her hope that others can be spared from the same fate. She lives in central Pennsylvania with her husband and their two cats.